20 DAYS *to Better Spelling*

BOOKS BY NORMAN LEWIS

30 Days to a More Powerful Vocabulary
  (*with Wilfred Funk*)
Power with Words
How to Read Better and Faster
Lewis English Refresher and Vocabulary Builder
How to Speak Better English
Word Power Made Easy
Rapid Vocabulary Builder
How to Get More Out of Your Reading
20 Days to Better Spelling

For Children

Vocabulary and Spelling
Journeys through Wordland

20 DAYS

to Better

Spelling

BY NORMAN LEWIS

HARPER & BROTHERS   PUBLISHERS   NEW YORK

20 DAYS TO BETTER SPELLING

To Mary, Margie, and Debbie

CONTENTS

Your 20-Day Program for Better Spelling

20 DAYS *to Better Spelling*

1

What This Book Can Do For You

English spelling is difficult — no one claims otherwise. But you will find that it is far from difficult to become an excellent speller.

Let me tell you this about English spelling —

It is, without a doubt, the most perplexing, most confusing, most paradoxical, most contradictory, and most frustrating system of putting letters together ever devised by man.

It is, indeed, exactly as the noted economist Thorstein Veblen once described it, probably in a moment of understandable exasperation —

"[It] satisfies," said Veblen, "all the requirements of the canons of reputability under the law of conspicuous waste. It is archaic, cumbrous, and ineffective."

It is the kind of system which caused Andrew Jackson, our seventh President, to make his famous and characteristic remark, also, doubtless, in a moment of justifiable pique —

Said Jackson, "It's a damned poor mind that can think of only one way to spell a word!"

But it is the system under which we operate — and perplexing, confusing, contradictory, and frustrating though it may be, if accurate spelling is your goal you have no choice but to come to terms with it.

You *can* come to terms with English spelling.

Indeed, you can do more than that. You can attain a considerable degree of skill and self-assurance — you can perhaps even come very close to complete mastery.

You can do all this through an intensive, carefully set up, and comprehensive training program.

Thorough and successful training in English spelling is probably far easier to achieve than you may realize; the time required is probably far less than you expect.

Do you consider yourself an incorrigibly poor, a practically hopeless speller? Within a short time after you start your training the improvement can be tremendous, the results almost spectacular.

Or do you, like so many educated people, feel that there are certain specific weaknesses, certain special areas of doubt and confusion in your spelling? A short period of intensive training can transform you into as nearly perfect a speller as it is humanly possible to be.

To become an efficient and self-confident speller of English words requires no unusual memory power; no more than average education and literateness; no greater ability to concentrate than most people normally have; and no special talent or flair for language.

All you need is a sound approach, the proper kind of training, and a sincere willingness to devote time and effort.

The sound approach and proper training you will find in this book —

The time and effort are up to you.

The Two Keynotes of Your Training Program

The broad base of your learning will involve a complete understanding of the fundamental principles under which English spelling operates, combined with an automatic adjustment, through memory-association devices, to the correct patterns of specially difficult demons.

This book aims, directly and primarily, to increase your spelling ability, to make you a far better, far more accurate speller, to eliminate most, if not all, of your *unconscious* errors, and to help you settle your doubts and confusions about commonly misspelled words.

But of perhaps even greater importance, this book offers you a special psychological dividend —

A dividend that comes from a rich and rewarding learning experience in a field where many people — perhaps you are among them — have had only failure and frustration —

A dividend that comes from a sound and intensive training program that will produce immediate and observable results.

For the *satisfaction* and *strong feeling of accomplishment* that result from successful training will play as effective a role in building your security and self-assurance in spelling as the training itself or the knowledge gained from such training.

Let me explain now, detail by detail and point by point, how this intensive training program sets up.

I. BASIC PRINCIPLES

Twenty-three main chapters in the book will discuss — slowly, methodically, clearly — the fundamental principles under which English spelling operates.

The *explanations* of these dry-as-dust principles will be our least concern — for such explanations, by themselves, are of negligible value and can be read (in their characteristic dry-as-dust language) in the introductory pages of any large dictionary.

What these twenty-three chapters will give you, by means of techniques and methods to be explained shortly, is thorough and intensive training in *applying the principles* to the solution of the kind of problems that incessantly plague the average speller —

Problems like:

When to double a consonant, and when to leave it alone.

Whether to end a word with *-ance* or *-ence*; *-able* or *-ible*; *-ary* or *-ery*; *-er* or *-or*; *-sy* or *-cy*, etc.

When to drop a final *-e* before adding a suffix, and when to retain it.

When to write *-ie*, and when to write *-ei*.

How to choose between *-cede*, *-ceed*, and *-sede*; between *-ise*, *-ize*, and *-yze*; between *-ly* and *-ally*; between *-efy* and *-ify*, etc., etc.

These comparatively few but crucial and constantly recurring problems account for over 90 per cent of the errors commonly made by educated adults — and efficient training in the basic principles of English spelling can eliminate every one of them.

You will not, I repeat, merely learn these principles —

Rather, you will be thoroughly trained to apply them successfully to the solution of recurrent problems —

You will completely understand them in all their various aspects and ramifications —

You will realize what's behind them, why they function as they do, where the exceptions and inconsistencies and irregularities come from.

You will thus recognize that despite the seeming lawlessness of spelling patterns there are at bottom broad and pervading conventions which govern the proper sequence of letters in English words.

And, as an inevitable result of training in the application of basic principles, you will shortly be able to make instantaneous, unconfused, and accurate decisions as to the correct patterns of most of the words which may now trouble you.

II. MNEMONICS (pronounced *ne-MON-iks*)

The *word* "mnemonics" may be new to you; but the *idea* behind the word is probably quite familiar.

Mnemonics are special aids to memory, memory tricks if you like, based on the theory of association.

It would be difficult and tiresome, for example, to memorize the exact number of days in every one of the twelve months — but the well-known rhyme *"30 days hath September, etc."* eliminates the need for painful and perhaps untrustworthy memorizing. The rhyme itself can be learned in a few seconds — and with the *mnemonic* in mind you can know instantaneously and correctly whether a month has 28, 30, or 31 days.

It would be equally tiresome to commit to memory the direction of the one-way traffic on each of the hundred-odd streets in New York City. So most New York motorists use a simple and effective *mnemonic*: *even*-numbered streets go *east*. The initial e's in *even* and *east* form an association device for quick and accurate remembering — in other words, a *mnemonic*.

Fifty-five special spelling demons, words that are particularly confusing even to the most literate of spellers (such as *embarassed* or *embarrassed?*, *anoint* or *annoint?*, *inoculate* or *innoculate?*, *dependant* or *dependent?*, *battalion* or *batallion?*, etc.), are discussed in the ten mnemonics chapters[1] of the book, each demon tied up to some sort of association device so that its correct pattern can be learned — permanently and unforgettably — in a few seconds.

The mnemonic for *embarrassed*, for example, is "two robbers were *embarrassed* in Sing Sing." The important problem in *embarrassed* is the number of r's and s's — the mnemonic (*two* robbers, Sing Sing) immediately and clearly demands two of each.

The mnemonic for *inoculate* is its synonym *inject*. The problem of how many n's and c's is settled at once — as in *inject*, only one of each.

The confusing problem of *batallion* or *battalion* is solved quickly by using the related word *battle* as a mnemonic. Like *battle*, *battalion* has two t's and one l.

Your training in mnemonics will give you immediate and effortless control over the most frequently misspelled words in the English

---

[1] These are inserted at random after various basic-principles chapters.

language. Five to ten of these words will be presented in each mnemonics chapter, and constant and repeated review of past demons and their association links in each succeeding mnemonics chapter will eventually make the correct pattern of these fifty-five trouble-some forms practically automatic in your writing.

You will be highly conscious of the mnemonic for each word only through the period of your training. The first half-dozen times you write *embarrassed, inoculate, battalion* or any of the other fifty-five demons, you will pause and say the mnemonic to yourself. After that first half-dozen times, you will be ready to give up the association devices as *conscious* aids. Then the mnemonics will begin to fade from your conscious thinking, for the correct patterns of the confusing words you have studied will have become a permanent part of your self-assured spelling reactions —

— As self-assured and lacking in doubt or hesitation as the patterns of simple forms like *cat* or *school* or *night* or *girl* or any other words which you now write correctly without second thought.

3

Two Special Techniques in Your Training

The success of your work with this book will depend on your use of the two indispensable techniques that train you to become *visually* and *muscularly* adjusted to correct spelling patterns. These techniques will make your new spelling habits permanent and automatic.

Learning is a complex activity.

It is of course basically intellectual, and in fields like mathematics, or literature, or English grammar, the purely intellectual processes are the predominating if not the exclusive factors to be reckoned with.

But other factors are also involved in many types of learning.

In learning to speak a foreign language, you have to develop a certain facility in the physical organs of speech in order to be able to reproduce the required accent; in learning a comparatively simple skill like typing or a fairly difficult one like surgery you must develop a high degree of manual dexterity; in learning to drive an automobile you must develop habits of instantaneous muscular responses, etc.

Foreign languages, typing, surgery, driving a motorcar — these are all real learning situations, and although intellectual development is at the base of each, there is still a good deal of physical or bodily learning that must go on before genuine skill can be acquired.

So also in spelling.

The foundation of mastering correct spelling patterns is of course intellectual — and this intellectual foundation will be emphasized by your training in basic principles and in the use of mnemonics.

7

But the attainment of genuine skill and self-assurance in spelling also requires a certain amount of visual and muscular re-education. Let me explain these two special techniques in your training.

I. SHARPENING YOUR VISUAL MEMORY

Visual memory is part of the human equipment — it is perhaps better developed in some people than in others, but every normal human being has a good, serviceable visual memory.

Your visual memory is a storehouse of familiar images. Owing to visual memory, you can recognize something or somebody you've previously seen without carefully examining every detail, you can instantaneously react to familiar words on a page of print without looking at every letter, you can immediately distinguish your wife from your mother-in-law without engaging in a feature-by-feature analysis, etc.

Visual memory for spelling patterns develops by itself over the years — but it is often a slow and long process. And all too frequently it does not grow in precisely the direction that is most helpful.

If in the course of your training program with this book you discover X words which you never realized you were misspelling, plus Y words which you were never really sure of, then there are at least X plus Y instances in which your visual memory did not cooperate with your needs. These X plus Y words probably came up in your reading with a certain frequency — but because, as is perfectly natural, you read for meaning and not for patterns, you saw the correct spellings but never formed a sufficiently strong visual impression to be able to reproduce the words accurately and confidently.

A very important part of your training, then, will be devoted to sharpening your visual memory of spelling patterns by showing you how to react strongly to the appearance of the crucial letters or areas in certain words — the letters that cause the most confusion, the areas where many spellers are tempted into error.

The crucial letters or areas of every troublesome word throughout the book will be printed in heavy black type, thus: **nie**ce; and by using the *visual-aid card*[1] you can form strong visual attachments where they will do you the most good.

---

[1] This will be found inserted near the front of the book.

Every important word discussed in the book is so printed that it will fit clearly within the window of the visual-aid card — and you will thus be able to examine the correct pattern without any distraction from surrounding print.

Pay particular attention to the heavy black letters of each word offered for visual training — these are the letters with which you will aim to gain the greatest visual intimacy, so that eventually any other combinations will look awkward, out-of-balance, and therefore unquestionably incorrect.

Such visual emphasis will start an unusual chain of circumstances. Having carefully examined a troublesome word through the window of the visual-aid card, you will be involuntarily on the alert for it in all your reading; and you will probably be somewhat startled to notice how often it occurs, how strongly it arrests the eye. Every time you meet it you will again be observing its correct spelling pattern, again driving a little deeper than before your visual adjustment to its proper appearance and especially to the correct combination of letters in its crucial area.

Do not discount the importance of this visual training — nothing can so quickly and effectively make you feel at home with correct spelling as frequently repeated and consciously directed visual experience with the proper patterns of difficult words. So let every word you work on during your training appear for ten to fifteen seconds within the window of the visual-aid card — this is one of the most valuable steps you can take toward attaining complete self-confidence and a high degree of accuracy in English spelling.

II. SHARPENING YOUR MUSCULAR OR "KINESTHETIC" MEMORY

In addition to your visual memory, your muscular or, as it is called technically, *kinesthetic* memory is an important factor in your mastery of English spelling.

Kinesthetic memory, like visual memory, is part of the human equipment. It is a storehouse of previous muscular activity and is well developed in every normal human being.

It is your kinesthetic memory that permits you to bring a glass to your lips without conscious direction from your brain. It is your kinesthetic memory that regulates more complex muscular activity such as that involved in typing, swimming, driving a motorcar, catching a ball, performing a surgical operation or writing a word correctly.

To use the visual-aid card for best results, hold it on a page so that the word under study fits evenly within the window. Examine the word, and particularly the heavy black letters, for ten to fifteen seconds; then push the card up so that the word is hidden, and reproduce the correct pattern on the blank line to the right of the word; finally pull the card down again so the word reappears in the window and compare what you've written with the printed pattern.

This is how the visual-aid card looks with a word showing through the window.

inoculate

But all these activities had to be slowly learned and, at first, consciously directed by the brain. When a muscular response has been performed frequently enough the muscles seem to do their own thinking, no conscious direction is required from the brain, the act has become reflexive and automatic.

By far the greatest proportion of words you now write are the result of automatic kinesthetic memory — you rarely stop on familiar, easily spelled words to figure out which letter comes after which.

But because it is so easy today, don't think it just happened. As a child you learned very carefully and consciously to write *cat* and *rat* and *night* and *light* — now the reaction is so customary that it has become automatic, your muscles respond as if of their own volition, almost as reflexively as in eating or swallowing or walking or raising your arm to ward off a blow.

In successful training, you will wish to store up in your kinesthetic memory the correct spelling patterns of all the troublesome and confusing words you meet, so that accurate muscular reactions eventually become as automatic as in writing the simple, easily spelled words you now know so well.

This, too, will not happen by itself — you will have to train for it.

Your kinesthetic training will go hand in hand with your visual training. Next to each important word in both the basic-principles and mnemonics chapters you will find a blank line. After you have examined the correct pattern of a word in the visual-aid window, noting particularly the heavy black letters, push the card up just enough to hide the word from view, then immediately, and with actual pen or pencil in hand, write the word in the blank provided for that purpose. Your muscles will be guided by the visual image you have retained, and you will begin to store up correct patterns in your kinesthetic memory.

You will find an opportunity to make a kinesthetic adjustment to the spelling pattern of every important word at least two and often three or more times within a single chapter. *Take advantage of every such opportunity.*

Your training program, then, takes three essential approaches to the development of a high order of skill in spelling:

1. *Intellectual:* Full understanding of fundamental principles combined with effective mnemonics for specially confusing words. This is the broad base of your training.

2. *Visual:* Thorough familiarity with the proper appearance of a word, with special emphasis on crucial letters.

3. *Kinesthetic:* Development of accurate and automatic muscular responses through the actual writing of a word a calculated number of times.

When you have made a full intellectual, visual, and kinesthetic adjustment, in that order, to the correct pattern of a troublesome word, the chances of your ever misspelling it through either carelessness or confusion will be practically negligible.

4

How to Use This Book to Best Advantage

You are almost ready, now, to start your training. Here are five important suggestions for making the time you spend in such training pay big dividends.

Let me repeat, for emphasis, something I have said in a previous chapter.

Namely, *that this training program on which you are about to embark can be a rich and rewarding learning experience.*

It can be rich and rewarding, it can give you a definite feeling of accomplishment, it can offer you a good deal of satisfaction and even pleasure — if you are willing to co-operate with it.

Let me, therefore, make some suggestions that will help you co-operate fully with the training this book offers, that will make it possible for you to gain a maximum of benefit and improvement.

SUGGESTIONS FOR GETTING THE MOST OUT OF THIS BOOK

1. *This is an intensive training program — so, for best results, work intensively at it.*

"Intensively" would mean, in respect to time, *between a half hour and an hour a day,* and as many days in the week as the circumstances of your life permit.

This schedule will make it possible for you to master the twenty-seven training and ten mnemonic chapters of the book in no more than *twenty actual working days* — less than a month from start to finish if you actively commit yourself to a program of at least five days a week.

Thirty minutes to an hour a day for only twenty days may sound like a phenomenally short period in which to develop into an efficient, self-assured, and accurate speller, but that is all the time you will need to become fully trained — provided you work intensively, carefully, patiently.

For personal reasons of your own, you may prefer to take a longer period or you may, on the other hand, find it possible to complete the program in less than twenty working days. That is of course up to you. To provide a reasonable and attainable goal, I have indicated throughout the book which chapters can comfortably be completed in each day of your training — but if you prefer to set up a time schedule better suited to your needs, by all means do so. *In any case, however, whether you follow the program I offer or the one you plan for yourself, make every effort to keep to your training methodically and as much as possible without interruptions or extensive time gaps.*

2. *Go slow.*

I have tried to keep the style of the book clear, light, and breezy — and so you may be tempted into quick and superficial reading. Keep in mind, however, that this is a book only in the physical sense. In actuality, it is not a book at all, but a training program, a classroom on paper; for maximum benefit, work slowly on every page, digest the material thoroughly, make sure you fully understand and can successfully apply all the material in one chapter before you go on to the next.

You will notice, as you proceed with your training, a good deal of calculated repetition, a deliberate step-by-step pace, constant summaries and recapitulations, and chance after chance to stop and practice. Suit your tempo to the demands of the program.

3. *Do not neglect to use the visual-aid card or to write each word when, and as often as, required.*

I have already explained the supreme importance of sharpening your visual and kinesthetic memory. To be a self-confident, accurate speller you need trained eyes and fingers as well as a trained mind. So keep a pen or pencil handy during all your sessions — and use it frequently. The more active a role you play, the more permanent your training will be.

4. *Take all tests as if in actual test situations.*

There are thirty-two chapter-end tests and four comprehensive review tests. To make self-checking simple and convenient, the answer to each question on all tests appears in parentheses directly to the right of the question. *Keep all answers concealed with the visual-aid card until you are ready to score the complete test.*

Take every test, and take it honestly. These tests will provide you with objective, unbiased reports on your progress. And study your results — if they are poor you are not working conscientiously enough. Allow for normal human frailty, of course — an occasional error here and there will be of no great significance. But consistently low scores on the tests will indicate the need for careful review of past material and a firm resolve to proceed more cautiously on new material.

5. *Do not skip around; do not dip in casually or at random.*

This is a training book, not a reading book. No matter how good a speller you consider yourself, you may find surprises on every page, you may discover that you were making errors you never realized. If you are firmly convinced that you are an expert on the material of a particular chapter, turn to the test to make sure. Only a perfect score would indicate that the chapter can be safely skipped.

All right — that gives you all the briefing you need.

These four chapters of lengthy but necessary introduction may have made the attainment of complete spelling efficiency and security seem to require effort and tenacity.

Perhaps it does — but the dividends will be well worth the investment.

You provide the time, the tenacity, and the effort — this book will do the rest.

5

(First Day)

How to Decide Between
-cede, -ceed, and -sede

PROBLEM
  super**cede**, super**ceed**, *or* super**sede**?

SOLUTION
  The problem of this chapter highlights the kind of troublesome
and confusing dilemma that so often confronts the speller of English words.

  It is typical of the vexatious decisions that have to be made so
frequently in even the most informal of writing.

  But like most other spelling problems, it can be solved quickly
and easily — once you understand and learn to apply basic principles.

  So let us examine the simple facts and basic principles behind
the spelling patterns of all the English words that end in the pronunciation *seed.*

  There are exactly a dozen such words, eleven of them in common
use, the twelfth somewhat obscure — all of them with final syllables
that are pronounced identically but spelled in three different ways:
-cede, -ceed, or *-sede.*

  To avoid doubt and confusion, to be able to make an instantaneous, self-assured, and accurate decision on the spelling of any
word whose final syllable is pronounced *seed,* you have to know
two facts.

Fact 1
  Of the twelve words, one, and only one, ends in the four letters
-S-E-D-E.

15

That one word is:

superrsede _____

Supersede, in fact, is the only word in the entire language with the *-sede* ending.

In short, *supersede* is unique.

And, as you will soon discover, unique spelling patterns are easy to remember. Because of their uniqueness, they stick in the mind like burs.

So you will have no further trouble with *supersede*.

How about the others?

You need be thoroughly familiar with three other words — three that are equally unique.

Fact 2

There are only three words in the language that end in the letters *-C-E-E-D.*

Namely:

succeed _____   proceed _____

exceed _____

These two facts, that only *supersede* ends in *-sede*, and that only *succeed, proceed,* and *exceed* end in *-ceed,* permit you to make an immediate and correct choice between *-sede, -ceed,* and *-cede.*

For, obviously, with two of the three possible spellings accounted for, the eight remaining words of the original twelve can end in only one way: *-C-E-D-E.*

There is no point, of course, in your learning these eight words so completely that you can reel them off in alphabetical order. But examine each one for a few seconds and become visually and kinesthetically adjusted to its required pattern.

1. accede _____   5. intercede _____

2. antecede _____   6. precede _____

3. cede _____   7. recede _____

4. concede _____   8. secede _____

How can you remember that *succeed, proceed,* and *exceed* belong in a class by themselves, and are not to be confused with the eight

-cede words? How can you fix these three crucial verbs permanently in your mind, nail them down for all time?

Consider:

Succeed starts with s.

Proceed starts with p, and means *go ahead.* (The importance of the meaning will be evident in a moment.)

Exceed starts with e.

Now think of the key phrase, *Full Speed Ahead.*

This one phrase, *Full Speed Ahead,* and in particular the word *speed,* will be your guarantee against two unpleasant possibilities, to wit:

1. Any annoying doubt as to whether a word correctly ends in *-ceed* or *-cede.*

2. Any error in writing *-cede* for *-ceed,* or vice versa.

Notice how simply this mnemonic works:

Speed ends in *-eed.*

The s of speed identifies **succeed.**

The p of speed identifies **proceed.**

The e of speed identifies **exceed.**

The ending of speed identifies the endings of all three words: succeed, proceed, exceed.

And finally, the word *ahead* in *Full Speed Ahead* identifies *proceed,* which means *go ahead,* eliminates *precede,* which means *come before.*

Think of *Full Speed Ahead,* and you automatically write **succeed,** **proceed** and **exceed** with the correct *-ceed* ending, all other words (except, of course, *supersede*) with the correct *-cede* ending.

This may sound complicated until you are used to it. It is actually quite simple. As with all mnemonics, you will consciously think of *Full Speed Ahead* when you have occasion to write one of the three *-ceed* words — for a time. Eventually, the mnemonic will fade from your mind — when you have such automatic control over the *seed* verbs that key phrases are no longer necessary.

And that's all there is to the problem of making a choice between *-cede, -ceed,* and *-sede.*

Except for one noteworthy irregularity.

Proceed, as you know, belongs to one of the three *-ceed* verbs.

But the noun and adjective forms do not follow suit.

Contrary to what you might normally expect, these forms are spelled:

procedure _____   procedural _____

Which, as you will eventually learn to accept, is not surprising.

Because the most normal thing in English spelling is the unexpected.

Let us now gather our information and start to formulate basic principles.

Point 1

Only one word in English ends in -*sede*, namely *supersede*.

Point 2

Only three words in English end in -*ceed*, namely *succeed*, *proceed*, and *exceed*. (Key: *Full Speed Ahead*.)

Point 3

All other words of similar sound end in -*cede*.

Point 4

Procedure and *procedural*, however, do not follow the pattern of *proceed*.

TEST YOURSELF

I. Decide on the correct ending (-*cede*, -*ceed*, or -*sede*) that attaches to each of the following roots, then write the complete word with that ending. (It is most important to rewrite the word, not merely add the required ending; for only by this means can you gain the kinesthetic and visual practice so essential for making correct patterns reflexive and automatic.) For your convenience, the proper endings appear in parentheses along the right margin of the page — keep them concealed with the visual-aid card until you are ready to check your learning.

1. ac— _____ (cede)

2. con— _____ (cede)

3. suc— _____ (ceed)

4. se— _____ (cede)

5. pro— _____ (ceed)

6. pre— _____ (cede)

7. re— _____ (cede)

8. ante— _____ (cede)

9. ex— _____ (ceed)

10. super— _____ (sede)

11. inter— _____ (cede)

II. Decide on the missing letter or letters, then rewrite the complete word.

1. proc—dure _____ (e)

2. proc—dural _____ (e)

3. c—de _____ (e)

4. proc—d _____ (ee)

5. prec—de _____ (e)

6. conc—ding _____ (e)

7. sec—ding _____ (e)

8. super—ding _____ (se)

9. super—ded _____ (se)

10. ex—d _____ (cee)

11. ex—ding _____ (cee)

12. suc—ding _____ (cee)

13. inter—ding _____ (ce)

14. ac—ding _____ (ce)

A Footnote on Supersede

As you go on with your work in this book, it will soon become apparent that most of the peculiarities of English spelling are due to the mongrel ancestry of our language.

Almost every word you use was born in some foreign land — England, Italy, Greece, France, Germany, Norway, Denmark, India, China, Japan, Spain, etc.

And in most cases we retain the exotic spelling of the import, while Americanizing the pronunciation.

Hence the strange pattern of *supersede*, the only word in our language with the -*sede* ending.

Supersede was born in Rome thousands of years ago. It comes from Latin *super*, above, and *sedeo*, to sit.

If one thing *supersedes* another, it figuratively, and by derivation, sits above it.

Supersede is the only verb in English that derives directly from Latin *sedeo*, to sit, hence the only word with the -*sede* termination. But many nouns and adjectives come *indirectly* from *sedeo* or one of its forms: *president*, one who sits before a group; *sedentary*, moving little, hence sitting, as in *sedentary occupation; session*, a sitting or meeting of a group of people; *sedate*, calm, hence sitting still, etc.

The eleven -*ceed* or -*cede* words in English, on the other hand, all derive ultimately from Latin *cedo*, go: *precede*, go or come before; *secede*, go away; *intercede*, go between; *proceed*, go ahead, etc.

This doesn't explain why *succeed, proceed,* and *exceed* end in -*ceed* while the others end in -*cede* — and unfortunately there is no sound explanation. As our language grew, certain words became set in certain patterns — and those are the patterns, for better or worse, that we're stuck with today.

A Footnote on Antecede

Antecede is the one obscure verb in the list of common "seed" forms. It is practically never heard in speech nor seen in writing, but it does exist, and I have therefore felt compelled to include it in the complete list of -*cede* words.

Antecede, composed of Latin *ante*, before, and *cedo*, go, means *go before* — exactly the same as *precede*, which is the word in common use. The noun form, *antecedent*, is a grammatical term describing a word that *goes before* some pronoun, as in *the man who came to dinner. Man* is the antecedent of *who*.

I admit that this information is of little, if any, practical use — but take it for what it's worth.

(First Day, continued)

PRETEST
1. occurence, occurrance, *or* occurrence?
2. superintendant *or* superintendent?
3. innoculate, inocculate, *or* inoculate?
4. indispensible *or* indispensable?
5. dependible *or* dependable?

MNEMONICS

1. (occu**rence**, occu**rrance**, *or* occu**rrence**?)
An effective mnemonic highlights the critical letters of a spelling demon, emphasizes the troublesome areas where the inefficient speller may be tempted into error. There are two problems in this word: (1) single or double r? (2) *-ence* or *-ance*? As soon as you realize that an OCCU**RRENCE** is a CU**RRENT** event, in a sense, you can conveniently solve both problems with a single mnemonic. CU**RRENT** is rarely if ever misspelled — if you can spell CU**RRENT** you can spell OCCU**RRENCE**, which has the same double r followed by e.

    Correct spelling: occu**rrence** _____

    Mnemonic: cu**rrent** event

2. (superintend**ant** *or* superintend**ent**?)
The troublesome area here is the final syllable: *-ant* or *-ent*? In an apartm**ent** house, why does the SUPERINTEND**ENT** come around to the front door on the first of every month? For the R**ENT** of course — and R**ENT** is the mnemonic that shows you the required ending.

    Correct spelling: superintend**ent** _____

    Mnemonic: **rent**

3. (**inn**oculate, inn**occ**ulate, *or* inoculate?)

As you can begin to see, one of the frequent decisions you have to make when you spell English words is whether to double a consonant or leave it alone. Here the important questions are: Single or double *n*? And single or double *c*?

The common misspelling contains, erroneously, either two *n*'s or two *c*'s and, as it happens, the correct pattern requires only one of each. An effective and easily remembered mnemonic should have some relation in meaning to the problem word, as well as highlighting the areas of difficulty. To gain complete control over in**o**culate, think of its synonym, **inj**ect, which, like in**o**culate, has only one *c* and one *n*.

Correct spelling: in**o**culate _____

Mnemonic: **inj**ect

4. (indispens**ible** *or* indispens**able**?)

5. (depend**ible**, *or* depend**able**?)

We have begun to attack some of the fundamental and constantly recurring problems in English spelling. Whether to end a word with -*ence* or -*ance*, whether to double a consonant or leave it alone, whether to use the suffix -*able* or -*ible* — these three are high, very high, on the list of decisions you have to make over and over again in a normal day of writing or typing. Eventually we shall explore, and you will finally master, every aspect and facet of these and other important problems. Meanwhile we need a quick mnemonic for these two frequently misspelled words. Realize that **able** workers are ordinarily both depend**able** and indispens**able**, and your decision can become an automatic one — both words end in -*able*.

Correct spelling: indispens**able** _____

                     depend**able** _____

Mnemonic: **Able** workers are depend**able**
                      and indispens**able**.

MNEMONICS CHART

Correct Pattern	*Mnemonic*
1. occu**rrence** _____	cur**rent** event
2. superintend**ent** _____	**rent**

Correct Pattern	Mnemonic
3. ino**c**ulate _____	**inject**
4. indispens**able** _____	**able** worker
5. depend**able** _____	**able** worker

A Footnote on Indispensable

Indispensable is far more often misspelled than its cousin *dependable* — indeed, it is the rare speller who writes *-able* after *indispens-* and is self-confident enough to think no further about it. And there is good and sound reason for this confusion — most English words with a root ending in *-ns* take the suffix *-ible: defensible, reprehensible, incomprehensible,* etc. But not *indispensable,* nor, of course, its affirmative form, *dispensable.*

While *dependable* is nowhere nearly so often misspelled, I have purposely included it in the same chapter with *indispensable* so that you can link the two words in your mind — *dependable* will help you remember *indispensable.*

Consider one more point —

Some few spellers tend to write inde**s**pens- instead of the correct indispens-. If you have, or think you may have, such a tendency, think of the related word di**s**pense, which is practically never misspelled.

TEST YOURSELF

I. Check the correct pattern.

1. (a) dependible,	(b) dependable	(b)
2. (a) occurrence,	(b) occurrance	(a)
3. (a) superintendant,	(b) superintendent	(b)
4. (a) indispensible,	(b) indispensable	(b)
5. (a) inoculate,	(b) innoculate	(a)

II. Recall the mnemonic for each word.

1. occu**rren**ce _____	(cu**rren**t event)
2. superintend**ent** _____	(**rent**)
3. ino**c**ulate _____	(inje**c**t)
4. indispens**able** _____	(**able** worker)
5. depend**able** _____	(**able** worker)

III. Decide on the missing crucial letter or letters, then rewrite the complete word.

1. depend—ble _dependable_____ (a)

2. occu—nce _occurrence_____ (rre)

3. superintend—nt _superintendent_____ (e)

4. indispens—ble _indispensable_____ (a)

5. i—o—ulate _____ (n,c)

How to Decide Between -ize,
-ise, and -yze

PROBLEMS
analize *or* analyze?
improvize *or* improvise?
surprize *or* surprise?
ostracize *or* ostracise?

SOLUTION
Good spelling is in large part dependent on visual memory, as I have said. If, by now, *supersede* at first glance looks familiar and proper to you while *supercede* or *superceed* looks odd and improper, then you have begun to rely on your visual memory.

Everyone has a visual memory. You have one — and it is probably well developed, as it is in most human beings.

You rely on your visual memory every day — by means of it you can distinguish between Uncle Egbert and Aunt Lizzie, between a bowl of mush and a porterhouse steak, between a kiddie car and a Cadillac convertible. The things I have mentioned contain gross differences and are easy to distinguish one from the other — but things which contain fine and minute differences are just as easy to distinguish.

For example, playing cards.

If you devote any time to card games, you are constantly sharpening your visual memory of the fine differences between, say, a king and queen of diamonds, or an ace of clubs and an ace of spades. When you pick up your hand for a bridge or canasta game you recognize the cards instantaneously and automatically, and you sort them out in whatever way is proper.

25

Sharpening, and learning to rely on, your visual memory is a basic and indispensable technique in the mastery of English spelling.

When you have sharpened your visual memory —

When you have learned to rely on visual memory to conquer certain confusing and easily misspelled words —

Then, without the slightest hesitation, you will be able to distinguish — instantaneously — a correct pattern from an incorrect pattern.

And you will be impelled — automatically — to accept the proper combination, to reject an improper one.

Most of your success in spelling today comes from an unconscious dependence on visual memory — which is as it should be. Visual memory is so valuable and effective a technique that I am going to help you depend on it to a greater and greater degree; I am going to show you how to develop it into a skill of a very high order.

Visual memory will be your means of successful attack on the words in this chapter.

These words belong to a group that cause the kind of headache no aspirin can cure.

There are over 450 of them — words whose final syllables sound exactly alike, but which may end in one of three ways:

1. -*ise*
2. -*ize*
3. -*yze*

Your first goal is to know, by visual assurance and without hesitation, which of the three endings to tack on to any of the 450 words you may have occasion to use.

And your final goal is to be able to react instantaneously, automatically, and accurately with the correct ending when you write any word in this group.

Does this sound like too formidable a task, too much to ask of one human being?

Actually there's nothing to it — it is simplicity itself.

For a knowledge of a few clear and foolproof principles, when combined with a sharpened visual memory, will give you full and self-confident control over all 450 of these perplexing words.

Point 5

Most of these confusing words end in *-ize*, the popular American ending. If you are ever in any real doubt, *-ize* is probably the safe form to use.

For example:

agon**ize**	caps**ize**
mechan**ize**	character**ize**
apolog**ize**	hypnot**ize**
minim**ize**	philosoph**ize**
appet**ize**	idol**ize**
alphabet**ize**	apolog**ize**
popular**ize**	modern**ize**
memor**ize**	organ**ize**

Don't become too involved with these *-ize* words. There are over 400 of them, and you need only remember that the mathematical probability of *-ize* being the correct ending is therefore very great.

Point 6

Two and only two common words end in *-yze*.[1]   These two are:

1. anal**yze** _____   2. paral**yze** _____

I repeat, only these two common words end in *-yze* — they are easy to remember and can at once be cleared out of the way.

Point 7

There are, finally, thirty-six common words that end in *-ise*. These are the words to become most intimate with. Be absolutely sure of these thirty-six, and of *analyze* and *paralyze*, and the problem vanishes — *all others end in -ize.*

Aha, you are thinking skeptically, how am I going to remember thirty-six words that end in *-ise*?

It is easier than it sounds.

To begin with, you spell many of them correctly now — for only a few of them are subject to frequent misspelling by literate citizens. That alone narrows the field considerably.

---

[1] There are a few other, highly technical, words that end in *-yze*, notably *dialyze, catalyze,* and *electrolyze* — but if you are sufficiently familiar with chemistry or physics to use these words you probably know how to spell them.

Furthermore, you are not planning to memorize them, but only to react to them visually, which is considerably simpler. You need never rattle off the thirty-six *-ise* words — your simple goal is to become visually familiar with them, so that an *-ize* ending on any of them looks improper and awkward.

And, finally, thirty of the thirty-six *-ise* words fall into natural groupings, so that only six are left in isolation.

Let us examine the thirty that fall into natural groupings.

Group I. Any Combination with "wise"

1. wise _____

2. sidewise _____

3. otherwise _____

4. likewise _____

5. contrariwise _____

etc.

Group II. Any Combination Ending in "-vise"

6. advise _____

7. supervise _____

8. revise _____

9. improvise _____

10. devise _____

(The reason here is that such words are built on the Latin root *visus*, to see.)

Group III. Any Combination Built on the Word "rise"

11. rise _____

12. moonrise _____

13. sunrise _____

14. uprise _____

15. arise _____

Note, please, that it is not the letter *r* which demands *-ise*, as words like *characterize, memorize,* and *popularize* show. It is a combination built on the actual word "rise" that counts.

Group IV. Any Common Words Ending in "-prise"

16. enterprise _____

17. apprise _____

18. reprise _____

19. surprise _____

20. comprise _____

(The obvious exception, of course, is *prize* itself, or any word built on it, such as *underprize* or *overprize*.)

Group V. Three Words and Only Three Ending in "-mise"

21. surmise _____   23. demise _____

22. compromise _____

Group VI. Five Special "-cise" Words

24. exercise _____   27. incise _____

25. excise _____   28. circumcise _____

26. exorcise _____

(Note that there are only five special -cise words. Others, like *ostracize, criticize, italicize*, etc., end in -cize. The reason for the special spelling of these five is that each comes from a Latin root containing an s— *incisus, to cut.*)

Group VII. Two "guise" Words

29. **guise** _____   30. disguise _____

These thirty, since they fall into groupings, will offer no real difficulty.

And, with thirty grouped, we have only six isolated -ise words to commit to visual memory.

These are:

31. advertise _____   34. merchandise _____

32. despise _____   35. franchise _____

33. chastise _____   36. enfranchise _____

So to attack the problem efficiently, you will take three simple steps for quick and successful learning.

Step 1

Become visually familiar with the two common -yze words:

   1. analyze _____   2. paralyze _____

Step 2

Study the thirty-six common -ise words, seeing them in groups, and gaining a strong visual impression of each one.

I. "-wise"

1. wise _____
2. sidewise _____
3. otherwise _____
4. likewise _____
5. contrariwise _____

II. "-vise"

6. advise _____
7. supervise _____
8. revise _____
9. improvise _____
10. devise _____

III. "rise"

11. rise _____
12. moonrise _____
13. sunrise _____
14. uprise _____
15. arise _____

IV. "-prise"

16. enterprise _____
17. apprise _____
18. reprise _____
19. surprise _____
20. comprise _____

V. "-mise"

21. surmise _____
22. compromise _____
23. demise _____

VI. "-cise"

24. exercise _____
25. excise _____
26. exorcise _____
27. incise _____
28. circumcise _____

VII. "-guise"

29. guise _____
30. disguise _____

VIII. Others

31. advert**ise** _____
34. merchand**ise** _____

32. desp**ise** _____
35. franch**ise** _____

33. chast**ise** _____
36. enfranch**ise** _____

Step 3

All others, and whenever in doubt, you will spell *-ize*.

That's all there is to it — I think you'll agree that it is simpler than it may have seemed at first.

TEST YOURSELF

Decide on the proper ending (*-ize*, *-ise* or *-yze*) for each of the following, then rewrite the complete word.

1. mechan— _____ (ize)
2. appet— _____ (ize)
3. critic— _____ (ize)
4. anal— _____ (yze)
5. paral— _____ (yze)
6. likew— _____ (ise)
7. adv— _____ (ise)
8. superv— _____ (ise)
9. rev— _____ (ise)
10. dev— _____ (ise)
11. Anglic— _____ (ize)
12. bapt— _____ (ize)
13. civil— _____ (ize)
14. ar— _____ (ise)
15. enterpr— _____ (ise)
16. appr— _____ (ise)

17. repr— _____ (ise)

18. surpr— _____ (ise)

19. compr— _____ (ise)

20. equal— _____ (ize)

21. general— _____ (ize)

22. moral— _____ (ize)

23. surm— _____ (ise)

24. comprom— _____ (ise)

25. dem— _____ (ise)

26. minim— _____ (ize)

27. legal— _____ (ize)

28. local— _____ (ize)

29. exerc— _____ (ise)

30. exc— _____ (ise)

31. exorc— _____ (ise)

32. inc— _____ (ise)

33. circumc— _____ (ise)

34. harmon— _____ (ize)

35. gu— _____ (ise)

36. disgu— _____ (ise)

37. emphas— _____ (ize)

38. advert— _____ (ise)

39. desp— _____ (ise)

40. chast— _____ (ise)

41. merchand— _____ (ise)

42. franch— _____ (ise)

43. enfranch— _____ (ise)

44. econom— _____ (ize)

45. modern— _____ (ize)

A Footnote on Forms

Analyze and *paralyze*, you now know, end in -yze. You will then have no trouble with the noun forms of these verbs, for you keep the y in its proper place, and otherwise spell according to sound.

analysis _____ paralysis _____

The letter y falls right in place, also, in forms like psychoanalyze, psychoanalysis, psychoanalyst, psychoanalytic (all preferably written as solid words, not hyphenated), paralytic, etc.

Whenever you have some doubt about the spelling of a difficult word, consider whether there is not some other form of the same word which you are sure of. If you can find such a related form, your problem is settled — use a similar pattern for the hard word.

This is so valuable a technique that we shall use it over and over in our mnemonics chapters.

MNEMONICS
Two

PRETEST
1. siege *or* seige?
2. sieze *or* seize?
3. batallion *or* battalion?
4. parallel *or* paralell?
5. fricassee *or* friccasee?

MNEMONICS

1. (siege *or* seige?)
2. (sieze *or* seize?)

One of the major problems in English spelling is how to make an accurate and self-assured choice between *ie* and *ei*.

In Chapters 8 and 9 we'll explore the question thoroughly, but at this point it will be interesting and instructive to consider the two contrasting and somewhat contradictory forms SIEGE and SEIZE.

(As you continue with your training, you will note how effectively the mind stores up contradictory spellings.)

A SIEGE is the surrounding of a fortified city by an enemy army — and therein lies our obvious mnemonic. An army lays SIEGE to, or BESIEGES, a CITY — the letter *i* in CITY reminds you to use *i* before E in SIEGE and BESIEGE.

On the other hand, it is common practice, in certain violent levels of society, to SEIZE one's enemy or adversary by the NECK — the vowel *e* in NECK reminds you to use *e* before *i* in SEIZE and SEIZURE.

I admit that this contrast is somewhat fanciful, as many mnemonics are — but because the phrases "SIEGE of a CITY" and "SEIZE by the NECK" present clear and striking pictures, the mnemonics, fanciful though they may be, are easy to remember and will provide

34

valuable aids in keeping straight on the proper combinations in SIEGE, BESIEGE, SEIZE, and SEIZURE.

Correct spellings: siege _____

besiege _____

seize _____

seizure _____

Mnemonics: besiege, or lay siege to, a city; seize by the neck.

3. (batallion *or* battalion?)

As we shall learn in a later mnemonics chapter, one of the simplest and most practical of association devices is to make a memory link between a perplexing form of a word and a form that virtually defies misspelling.

To settle once and forever the question of how many *t*'s and *l*'s occur in the word under discussion, link it to its easily spelled form BATTLE. Everyone can spell BATTLE — and BATTLE, with its obvious two *t*'s and one *l*, immediately shows the correct combination in BATTALION.

Correct Spelling: battalion _____

Mnemonic: battle

4. (paralell *or* parallel?)

820675

Here we have another major spelling problem — when to double a consonant and when to leave it alone.

If you link the test word to the phrase "**ALL** tracks are PAR-**ALL**EL," you will avoid any hesitation and doubt as to which *l* requires doubling — make sure that the word **ALL** appears in PAR-**ALL**EL and your problem is automatically and correctly solved.

Correct Spelling: parallel _____

Mnemonic: all tracks are parallel

5. (fricassee *or* friccasee?)

For this type of cooking, think of CASSEROLE, a word which does not tempt to misspelling. FRICASSEE can be made in a CASSEROLE, and, like CASSEROLE, has one c, two s's.

Correct Spelling: fricassee _____

Mnemonic:　　　　**cass**erole
　　　　　　　　　　———————

MNEMONICS CHART

Correct Pattern	*Mnemonic*
1. **si**ege _____	lay **si**ege to, or
2. be**si**ege _____	be**si**ege, a **ci**ty
3. **sei**ze _____	**sei**ze by the neck
4. ba**tt**alion _____	ba**tt**le
5. pa**rall**el _____	**all** tracks are pa**rall**el
6. fri**cass**ee _____	**cass**erole

TEST YOURSELF

I. Check the correct pattern.

1. (a) siege,	(b) seige	(a)
2. (a) besiege,	(b) beseige	(a)
3. (a) sieze,	(b) seize	(b)
4. (a) siezure,	(b) seizure	(b)
5. (a) batallion,	(b) battalion	(b)
6. (a) parallel,	(b) paralell	(a)
7. (a) friccasee,	(b) fricassee	(b)

II. Recall the mnemonic for each word.

1. **si**ege _____	(city)
2. be**si**ege _____	(city)
3. **sei**ze _____	(neck)
4. ba**tt**alion _____	(battle)
5. pa**rall**el _____	(**all** tracks)
6. fri**cass**ee _____	(**cass**erole)
7. superintend**ent** _____	(**rent**)
8. in**o**culate _____	(**inject**)

✓ 9. indispens**able** _____   (**able** worker)

10. depend**able** _____   (**able** worker)

11. occu**rrence** _____   (cu**rrent** event)

III. Decide on the missing crucial letters, then rewrite the complete word.

1. indispens—ble _____   (a)

2. depend—ble _____   (a)

3. occu—nce _____   (rre)

4. i—o—ulate _____   (n,c)

5. superintend—nt _____   (e)

6. s—ge _____   (ie)

7. bes—ge _____   (ie)

8. s—ze _____   (ei)

9. ba—a—ion _____   (tt,l)

10. para—e— _____   (ll,l)

11. fri—a—ee _____   (c,ss)

7

How to Decide Between *mis-* and *miss-*, *dis-* and *diss-*

PROBLEMS

misspelling *or* mispelling?

ishapen *or* misshapen?

dissapear *or* disappear?

dissapoint *or* disappoint?

dissatisfaction *or* disatisfaction?

SOLUTION

Practically no literate speller writes *miss-* at the beginning of a word that correctly starts with *mis-*.

Somehow, in English, there is little temptation to double the *s* in this prefix.

On the contrary, the tendency is the other way around. Among a goodly proportion of spellers, a certain number of crucial words which correctly start with *miss-* are incorrectly written with a single *s*.

Six such words are particularly troublesome:

1. misspell _____
2. misstate _____
3. misspend _____
4. misstep _____
5. misspeak _____
6. misshape _____

The poor speller, humanly if not logically, is likely to omit one of the two required *s*'s in each of these words.

Why, in all logic, do we need that second *s*?

Consider:

The basic roots of these words are:

1.	spell	4.	step
2.	state	5.	speak
3.	spend	6.	shape

And to this basic root, in each case, is added the negative prefix *mis-*, an old English form meaning *bad(ly)*, *wrong(ly)*, etc.

Thus:

1. *mis-* + spell = mis**s**pell: *spell wrongly*
2. *mis-* + state = mi**s**state: *state incorrectly*
3. *mis-* + spend = mi**ss**pend: *spend unwisely*
4. *mis-* + step = mi**ss**tep: *bad step*
5. *mis-* + speak = mi**ss**peak: *speak wrongly*
6. *mis-* + shape = mi**ss**hape: *shape badly*

In short, then —

When a root word starts with *s*, such as *spelling* or *shapen*, the addition of the negative prefix *mis-* will result in a double *s*: *misspelling*, *misshapen*, etc.

Most root words to which the prefix *mis-* will be added do not start with *s*. Hence they will contain a single, not a double, *s*.

As in:

mis- + apprehend = misapprehend
mis- + take = mistake
mis- + hap (from happen) = mishap
mis- + construe = misconstrue
etc.

And some few words beginning with *miss-* are not built on a negative prefix, but contain a double *s* for some other reason. These words are rarely misspelled, however, and offer no problem. Merely to complete the record, I will list some common *miss-* words below, none of which contain a negative prefix.

missile
missing, etc.
missive
mission, missionary, commission, admission, permission, etc.
Mississippi
Missouri

(The last two words come from Indian names; the first four are from the Latin root *missus*, to send, hence the double *s*.)

Your problems will arise only on the forms of the six crucial words which contain a root beginning with *s* and which add the negative prefix *mis-*.

    misspell _____   misspent _____

    misstate _____   misspeak _____

    misstep _____   misshapen _____

Understand the reason for the double *s* in these words, imprint their correct patterns on your visual memory, adjust to them kinesthetically — and the problem of whether to write *mis-* or *miss-* is one you will be able to solve without doubt or hesitation.

Now with *dis-* or *-diss*, on the other hand, we have a somewhat different problem.

There is a tendency, I have said, to use *mis-* where *miss-* is required.

Contrarily, there is an equally strong tendency to substitute an incorrect *diss-* for the required *dis-*.

Here again, confusion can be quickly and permanently eliminated by a clear understanding of basic principles —

And accurate, automatic reactions can be established through visual and kinesthetic training.

Like *mis-*, *dis-* is a prefix that attaches to a root form —

And, as in the case of *mis-* or *miss-*, the number of *s*'s is determined by whether or not the root itself starts with the letter *s*.

If the root starts with *s*, the complete word will contain a double *s*.

For example:

    dis- + satisfy = dissatisfy _____

    dis- + similar = dissimilar _____

    dis- + service = disservice _____

But if the root does *not* start with *s*, the complete word will *not* contain a double *s*.

For example:

   dis- + appear = di**s**appear _____

   dis- + appoint = di**s**a**pp**oint _____

   dis- + approve = di**s**a**pp**rove _____

   dis- + connect = di**s**connect _____

   dis- + agree = di**s**agree _____

Now let us explore these two points thoroughly.

Eliminating obscure words that appear only in the unabridged dictionary, and which you would probably have no occasion to write, there are exactly nineteen different words, no more, that start with *diss-*. All others (and there are over twelve columns of such words in the dictionaries) start with *dis-*.

There is no need to memorize these nineteen *diss-* words, but if you completely understand how each one of them is engineered on the principle of a combination of the prefix *dis-* plus a root starting with *s* you can eliminate all possible confusion between these nineteen *diss-* words and the two-hundred odd *dis-* words.

Let us examine the nineteen forms one by one, noting in each case how the root starts with *s*.

1. DI**SS**ATISFY _____
The root is **S**ATISFY, the prefix has a negative force. Other forms, such as *dissatisfied, dissatisfaction, dissatisfactory,* etc., are of the same pattern.

2. DI**SS**ECT _____
-**S**ECT is the Latin root *to cut;* the prefix *DIS-* in this instance means *apart;* hence DI**S**SECT is to cut apart. (Similarly *bisect* is to cut in two, *trisect,* cut in three; *intersect,* cut between, etc.)

3. DI**SS**EMBLE _____
The root is -**S**EMBLE, to appear, and is found in *semblance, resemble,* etc. *DIS-* again has a negative force, so that DI**SS**EMBLE means to pretend, to disguise, in other words to appear other than in actuality.

4. DI**SS**EMINATE _____
-**S**EMINATE comes from a Latin root *semen,* seed; the prefix *DIS-* means *in every direction.* So DI**SS**EMINATE, by derivation,

signifies *to scatter seeds in every direction* or *to scatter ideas widely*. A *seminary*, from the same root, is a place where seeds of knowledge are planted in the minds of students.

5. DISSENT _____

-SENT is a root meaning *to feel* or *think*, from which also derive *sentiment, sensation, sensual, sensible*, etc. *DIS-* in this case means *differently*, so to DISSENT is *to feel differently*, hence *disagree*. The noun DISSENSION follows the same pattern.

6. DISSERTATION _____

From -SERERE, to join. A DISSERTATION is a joining of words to discuss a subject apart (*DIS-*) from other subjects. The same root -*serere* also is found in *assert*.

7. DISSERVICE _____

Obviously SERVICE plus the negative *DIS-*.

8. DISSEVER _____

SEVER means *to separate;* to DISSEVER is *to separate apart.*

9. DISSIDENT _____

The root -SID is related to the SEDERE, *to sit,* which you will recall from *supersede*. A DISSIDENT sits apart from the rest of the group, in a manner of speaking.

10. DISSIMILAR _____

SIMILAR plus *DIS-*.

11. DISSIMULATE _____

This word has the same root as SIMILAR, Latin *simil*, like: to DISSIMULATE is to *disguise*, or *make unlike*.

12. DISSIPATE _____

This is one of the ten most frequently misspelled words in the language. The root is -SIP, to throw, plus *DIS-*, in every direction. So, when you DISSIPATE, you scatter your resources in every direction, often by sensual indulgence. This word has three danger spots — the double *s*, the following *i*, and the single *p*; and the understanding of the architecture of the word (DIS- + SIP, to throw) takes care of all three simultaneously.

13. DISSOCIATE _____

DIS- plus ASSOCIATE, with the first two letters omitted from the root, so actually *DIS-* plus -SOCIATE.

14. DI**SS**OLVE _____
DIS- plus the Latin root -**S**OLV, to loosen.

15. DI**SS**OLUBLE _____
The adjective form of DI**SS**OLVE has, strangely enough, the same meaning as **S**OLUBLE, the root to which *DIS-* is added.

16. DI**SS**OLUTE _____
Formed by adding *DIS-* to another spelling of Latin **S**OLV-, to loosen. A DI**SS**OLUTE character is morally loose, evil, wicked. The noun DI**SS**OLUTION means a loosening up of all connections, so that everything falls apart, as in *the dissolution of the industrial empire.*

17. DI**SS**ONANCE _____
DIS-, differently, plus **S**ONARE, to sound. DI**SS**ONANCE, then, is a combination of inharmonious sounds. *Resonant, unison, consonant,* and *sonorous* are all built on the same root, *sonare,* to sound.

18. DI**SS**UADE _____
The root found in *persuade* (-*suadere,* to urge) plus *DIS-*, against.

19. DI**SS**YLLABLE _____
This is the word **S**YLLABLE plus *DIS-*, two — hence a word of two syllables.

You can now combine your knowledge of the architecture of these nineteen words with visual memory to be able to recall, instantly, whether a *dis-* word belongs among the nineteen (and hence starts with *diss-*) or among the two hundred (and hence starts with *dis-*).

For further practice, examine the following chart. Make no attempt to memorize the nineteen *diss-* words. Instead, take three simple steps:

1. Understand how each *diss-* word is built —

2. Let the proper appearance register sharply on your visual memory —

3. Make a kinesthetic adjustment by writing each word in the space provided.

1. (DI**S** **S**ATISFY)   di**ss**atisfy _____

2. (DI**S** **S**ECT, cut)   di**ss**ect _____

3. (DIS SEMBLE, seem)   dissemble _____

4. (DIS SEMEN, seed)   disseminate _____

5. (DIS SENT, feel)   dissent _____

6. (DIS SERERE, join words)   dissertation _____

7. (DIS SERVICE)   disservice _____

8. (DIS SEVER, separate)   dissever _____

9. (DIS SID, sit)   dissident _____

10. (DIS SIMILAR)   dissimilar _____

11. (DIS SIMIL, like)   dissimulate _____

12. (DIS SIP, throw)   dissipate _____

13. (DIS SOCIATE)   dissociate _____

14. (DIS SOLV, loosen)   dissoluble _____

15. (DIS SOLV, loosen)   dissolve _____

16. (DIS SOLV, loosen)   dissolute _____

17. (DIS SONARE, sound)   dissonance _____

18. (DIS SUADERE, urge)   dissuade _____

19. (DIS SYLLABLE)   dissyllable _____

Once you have taken these three steps, you may be assured of one thing: You will never again be confused about whether to write *dis-* or *diss-* at the beginning of a word. And if you think you might wonder whether to use *dys-*, be assured on that count also: Only two common words start with *dys-*.

dysentery _____

dyspeptic _____

So let us now review the basic principles under which we have been operating.

Point 8

If a root starts with s, the addition of the prefix *mis-* or *dis-* will result in a double s — MISSPELLING, MISSTEP, DISSECT, DISSIPATE, etc.

Point 9

But if a root does not start with s, the addition of the prefix *mis-* or *dis-* will result in only a single s — MISAPPREHENSION, MISAPPLY, DISAPPEAR, DISAPPOINT, etc.

TEST YOURSELF

I. Attach the prefix *mis-* to the following roots, rewriting the complete words in the spaces provided.

1. spelling _____ (misspelling)

2. statement _____ (misstatement)

3. step _____ (misstep)

4. spent _____ (misspent)

5. shapen _____ (misshapen)

6. spoken _____ (misspoken)

7. hap _____ (mishap)

8. apprehend _____ (misapprehend)

9. construe _____ (misconstrue)

II. Attach the prefix *dis-* to the following roots, rewriting the complete words in the spaces provided.

1. appear _____ (disappear)

2. section _____ (dissection)

3. appoint _____ (disappoint)

4. -sent _____ (dissent)

5. approve _____ (disapprove)

6. -sertation _____ (dissertation)

7. agree _____ (disagree)

8. -sever _____ (dissever)

9. allow _____ (disallow)

10. -sidence _____ (dissidence)

11. appearance _____ (disa**pp**earance)

12. service _____ (di**ss**ervice)

13. -aster _____ (di**s**aster)

14. -semble _____ (di**ss**emble)

15. reputable _____ (di**s**reputable)

16. similarity _____ (di**ss**imilarity)

17. -sipate _____ (di**ss**i**p**ate)

18. solve _____ (di**ss**olve)

19. pleasure _____ (di**sp**leasure)

20. -seminate _____ (di**ss**eminate)

21. satisfy _____ (di**ss**atisfy)

22. simulate _____ (di**ss**imu**l**ate)

23. integrate _____ (di**s**integrate)

24. soluble _____ (di**ss**oluble)

25. embark _____ (di**s**embark)

26. -solute _____ (di**ss**olute)

27. credit _____ (di**s**credit)

28. like _____ (di**s**like)

29. -sonance _____ (di**ss**onance)

30. syllable _____ (di**ss**yllable)

31. connect _____ (di**s**connect)

32. entangle _____ (di**s**entangle)

33. -sociate _____ (di**ss**ociate)

34. -suade _____ (di**ss**uade)

35. comfort _____ (di**s**comfort)

(Third Day, continued)

PRETEST
1. persist**ant** *or* persist**ent**?
2. insist**ant** *or* insist**ent**?
3. depend**ant** *or* depend**ent**?
4. emba**ra**ssed *or* emba**rra**ssed?
5. a**n**oint *or* a**nn**oint?

MNEMONICS

A mnemonic, as you know, highlights the "danger spot" of a word.

It ties up, by some meaningful association, the "area of error," the place where most people go wrong, with some easily spelled word or with some logically connected phrase or idea, in such a way that the correct pattern of a difficult word is immediately clear.

You will recall that:

— in *occurrence*, the crucial letters are *-rre*, and the mnemonic *current event* helps avoid any possibility of error.

— in *superintendent*, the mnemonic *rent* highlights the correct ending.

— in *inoculate*, the mnemonic *inject* focuses attention on the single *n* and single c.

— in *dependable* and *indispensable*, the mnemonic *able worker* indicates the proper spelling of the final syllable, *-able*.

The words on which you have tested yourself in this chapter also lend themselves to quick learning through clear-cut, easily recalled mnemonics.

1. (persist**ant** *or* persist**ent**?)
2. (insist**ant** *or* insist**ent**?)
3. (depend**ant** *or* depend**ent**?)

-Ant or *-ent?* This is a question that causes considerable confusion and unhappiness, a question that constantly plagues the
inefficient speller.   Unfortunately there are no broad rules, no
sweeping generalizations that can immediately separate the sheep
from the goats, no way of keeping the *-ant* words from getting mixed
up with the *-ent* words.[1]

Four words are among those that cause particular trouble: superintend**ent**, persist**ent**, insist**ent** and depend**ent**— and one mnemonic
covers all four.

You recall that the superintend**ent** of an apartm**ent** house collects
the r**ent**. He is generally persist**ent** and insist**ent** about it and his
job is often depend**ent** on his success. Now these statements may
or may not constitute sound psychology, economics, or sociology—
no matter. Some mnemonics, as you will shortly discover, can be
weird to an outrageous degree, but if there is some relationship in
meaning and spelling between a mnemonic and a problem word,
truth and soundness and sanity are of secondary importance.

So simply get a picture in your mind of a superintend**ent** collecting
r**ent**, being persist**ent** and insist**ent**, and feeling that his job is
depend**ent** on his collections, and you have permanently mastered
four words that are frequently misspelled.

Needless to say, all forms of these words follow a similar pattern:

superintend**ence** _____   depend**ence** _____

persist**ence** _____   depend**ency** _____

insist**ence** _____   independ**ence** _____

And notice the contrast between depend**able**, undepend**able** and
depend**ent**, independ**ent**. With the letter *a* preceding *-ble*, you might
not expect a sudden change of vowel before *-nt*. Remember, however, that the unexpected is highly normal in English spelling.

Correct Spellings: persist**ent** _____

insist**ent** _____

depend**ent** _____

Mnemonic: **rent**

[1]Chapter 26 will explore the problem of *-ant*, *-ent*, *-ance*, *-ence* in all its
aspects and will explain why visual training is the most efficient solution.

4. (emba**ra**ss**ed** *or* emba**rr**a**ss**ed?)

Here the crucial question is the number of *r*'s and *s*'s. Most people misspell the word by using only one *r*, but every possible combination can occasionally be found. Consider this sentence: "**Two r**obbers were emba**rr**a**ss**ed when they were sent to **S**ing **S**ing [a New York State penitentiary]."

> **Two r**obbers — two *r*'s
> **S**ing **S**ing — two *s*'s

For a small percentage of spellers, the third syllable of *embarrassed* is a second area of difficulty — there is a temptation to suit the spelling to the sound and write *-ess*. If you are similarly tempted, think of this sentence: "When you're embarr**ass**ed, you feel like an **ass**."

All forms of this word follow the same pattern.

emba**rr**a**ss**ment _____   emba**rr**a**sses** _____

emba**rr**a**ss**ing _____   emba**rr**a**ss** _____

> *Correct Spelling:* emba**rr**a**ss**ed _____

> *Mnemonics:*   **Two r**obbers emba**rr**a**ss**ed in **S**ing **S**ing;
> feel like an **ass**.

5. (a**n**oint *or* a**nn**oint?)

The important letter in anoint is the single *n* following the *a*. (Whenever the word is misspelled, as it often is, a double *n* is erroneously used.) When someone is a**n**ointed, a**n o**il is generally used.

So:

> **an o**il — a**n**oint

(As you go on with your study of words you will begin to group those of similar difficulty. *Anoint* with one *n* will remind you of *inoculate* with one *n*.)

MNEMONICS CHART

Correct Pattern	*Mnemonic*
persist**ent** _____	**r**ent
insist**ent** _____	**r**ent

Correct Pattern	Mnemonic
depend**ent** _____	**rent**
emba**rr**a**ss**ed _____	**two r**obbers in Sing Sing; **ass**
a**no**int _____	a**n o**il

A Footnote on Embarrassment

The suffix -*ment* is added to a verb to form a noun. It is usually added to the verb as is, with no additions. For example, *embezzlement, encouragement, entanglement, advertisement,* etc. As you see, many verbs end in the letter *e,* and so -*ement* is a common and reputable ending.

But *embarrass* does not end in *e,* so there is no *e* after the -*ss* of *embarrassment.* (The incorrect pattern, *embarrassement,* is frequently found in unsophisticated writing.) *Embarrassment* belongs in the same class as *accomplishment, bewilderment, enlightenment,* etc. — no *e* at the end of the verb, no *e* preceding the -*ment.*

So watch your step on *embarrass* and its various forms — there are more temptations to go wrong than confront a newly landed sailor with all his back pay in his pocket.

TEST YOURSELF

I. Check the correct pattern.

1.	(a) persistant,	(b) persistent	(b)
2.	(a) insistant,	(b) insistent	(b)
3.	(a) dependant,	(b) dependent	(b)
4.	(a) embarassed,	(b) embarrassed	(b)
5.	(a) anoint,	(b) annoint	(a)

II. Recall the mnemonic for each word.

1. occu**rr**ence _____ (**current** event)

2. superintend**ent** _____ (**rent**)

3. in**o**culate _____ (**inject**)

4. indispens**able** _____ (**able** worker)

5. depend**able** _____ (**able** worker)

6. si**e**ge _____ (**city**)

  7. se**i**ze _____ (n**e**ck)

  8. ba**tt**alion _____ (ba**tt**le)

  9. par**all**el _____ (**all** tracks)

10. fri**c**a**ss**ee _____ (**cass**erole)

11. persist**ent** _____ (**rent**)

12. insist**ent** _____ (**rent**)

13. depend**ent** _____ (**rent**)

14. emba**rrass**ed _____ (**two r**obbers,
                                                                Sing Sing, **ass**)

15. an**oi**nt _____ (a**n oi**l)

III. Decide on the missing letter or letters, then rewrite the complete word.

  1. persist—nt _____ (e)

  2. insist—nt _____ (e)

  3. depend—nt _____ (e)

  4. emba—ed _____ (rrass)

  5. a—oint _____ (n)

  6. persist—nce _____ (e)

  7. insist—nce _____ (e)

  8. depend—nce _____ (e)

  9. depend—ncy _____ (e)

10. independ—nce _____ (e)

11. superintend—nce _____ (e)

12. emba—ment _____ (rrass)

13. a—ointed _____ (n)

14. emba—ing _____ (rrass)

15. occu—nce _____ (rre)

16. superintend—nt _____ (e)

17. i—o—ulate _____ (n,c)

18. depend—ble _____ (a)

19. undepend—ble _____ (a)

20. indispens—ble _____ (a)

21. bes—ge _____ (ie)

22. s—zure _____ (ei)

23. ba—a—ion _____ (tt,l)

24. para—e— _____ (ll,l)

25. fri—a—ee _____ (c,ss)

8

(Fourth Day)

How to Decide Between *ie* and *ei* in Long Syllables

PROBLEMS

   receive *or* recieve?
   niece *or* neice?
   inviegle *or* inveigle?
   seize *or* sieze?

SOLUTION

You have no doubt heard of the ingenious veteran of many a spelling battle. Despairing of ever straightening himself out on whether to use *ei* or *ie*, he evolved a plan which was practically foolproof. When he had to write a word like *receive* (or *recieve*?), *believe* (or *beleive*?), *achieve* (or *acheive*?), etc., he would make the e and i look identical, and place the dot squarely between them, as follows:

That is admittedly as good a way as any to cover up one's ignorance and avoid getting into trouble. But, actually, to learn, once and for all, when to write *ie* and when to write *ei* is so simple that it is unnecessary to descend to subterfuge, however successful.

There is, for example, the mnemonic rhyme that every school boy knows:

I before E
Except after C
Or when sounded like A
As in *neighbor* or *weigh.*

This is a good, reliable principle, provided you are aware of the possibility of exceptional cases.

Of the hundred or more English words which contain the combination *ie* or *ei* with the sound of *long-E-as-in-grief,* all but seventeen are covered by the *first two lines* of the jingle; and those pronounced with *long-A-as-in-weigh* are completely covered by the *last two lines* of the jingle.

But let's not go too fast.

We know that if the sound of the combination is *long-E-as-in-grief,* the proper pattern is *ie* after any letter *except c.*
For instance:

bel**ie**ve _____	rel**ie**ve _____
gr**ie**ve _____	p**ie**ce _____
ach**ie**ve _____	pr**ie**st _____
f**ie**nd _____	br**ie**f _____
f**ie**ld _____	shr**ie**k _____
y**ie**ld _____	gr**ie**f _____
s**ie**ge _____	th**ie**f _____
p**ie**r _____	cash**ie**r _____
p**ie**rce _____	rab**ie**s _____
n**ie**ce _____	front**ie**r _____

And we know that if the immediately preceding letter is *c,* the correct combination is *ei.*
For instance:

re**cei**ve _____	con**cei**ve _____
re**cei**pt _____	con**cei**t _____
ceiling _____	precon**cei**ve _____

de**ceive** _____   per**ceive** _____

de**ceit** _____   etc.

This is so simple, we need spend no further time on it: generally *ie*, but after the letter *c, ei*. (Remember, however, that we are considering only those words in which the *ie* or *ei* combination has the sound of *long-E-as-in-grief*.)

I have said that all but seventeen words with the sound of *long-E-as-in-grief* are covered by the first two lines of the traditional jingle.

What about the seventeen nonconformists?

These seventeen present no insuperable problem.

One of them is in a class by itself. Despite the immediately preceding *c*, the *ie* combination is used. This lone and unique rebel is:

1. finan**cier** _____

Seven others are most important. *Although there is no immediately preceding c, the ei combination is nevertheless used.* These words merit study; they are often misspelled.

2. s**ei**ze _____   6. w**ei**rd _____

3. s**ei**zure _____   7. w**ei**r (a river dam) _____

4. l**ei**sure _____   8. inv**ei**gle (Pronounced either *in-VEE-g'l* or *in-VAY-g'l*)

5. sh**ei**k _____   _____

Two others belong with the preceding seven, but are rarely misspelled:

9. **ei**ther _____   10. n**ei**ther _____

Three more are terms from chemistry:

11. cod**ei**ne[1] _____   13. caff**ei**ne[1] _____

12. prot**ei**n[1] _____

[1]Popular pronunciation gives each of these words a two-syllable pronunciation, with the long *e* sound in the second syllable. Many dictionaries, however, suggest a rarely heard three-syllable pronunciation.

And the last four are proper names:

14. Keith _____   16. Neil _____

15. Reid _____   17. O'Neill _____

Of these seventeen, then, seven require special study — these cause the most confusion:

seize _____   leisure _____

seizure _____   weird _____

sheik _____   weir _____

inveigle ____ _____

Commit these seven to visual memory, be aware of the other ten exceptional cases, and keep in mind that otherwise the jingle operates. You have then mastered *ie-ei* combinations in all words with the sound of *long-E-as-in-grief*.

To recapitulate the basic principle under which the words of this chapter have thus far operated, let us formulate:

Point 10

In words with the sound of *long-E-as-in-grief*, *ie* is the general combination, with *ei* the required pattern directly after the letter *c* — in all but seventeen special cases.

And now let us consider the last two lines of the jingle:

> Or when sounded like A
> As in *neighbor* or *weigh*.

This part of the mnemonic is 100 per cent trustworthy — if the sound of the combination is *long-A-as-in-neighbor-or-weigh*, the pattern is always *ei*.

For example:

neigh _____   skein _____

weigh _____   chow mein _____

weight _____   vein _____

freight _____   inveigh _____

rein _____   inveigle _____
                                   (pronounced *in-VAY-g'l* or
reign _____   *in-VEE-g'l*)

veil _____   heinous _____
                                   (pronounced *HAY-nus*)

However, the jingle does not go quite far enough; *ei* is also the correct combination for the sound of *long-I-as-in-height*. For example:

height _____   Fahrenheit _____

sleight _____   kaleidoscope _____
   (of hand)
                                      seismic (pronounced
gneiss _____   *SIZE-mic*) _____
   (a form of rock;
   pronounced *NICE*)   seismograph _____

stein (of beer)   leitmotif _____
                                         (a musical term; pronounced
_____   *LYTE-mo-teef*)

There are, as it happens, three important exceptions to the principle that the sound of *long-I-as-in-height* is spelled *ei* rather than *ie*. These special cases, rarely misspelled, are:

   fiery _____   hierarchy _____

   hieroglyphic _____

So we also operate under the following basic principle:

Point 11

In words with the sound of *long-A-as-in-neighbor* or *long-I-as-in-height,* *ei* is the correct combination in all but three special cases — *fiery, hieroglyphic, hierarchy.*

Your decision between *ie* and *ei* in long syllables is governed, then, by five simple rules —

   1. For *long-E-as-in-grief,* use *ie* generally
   2. Change to *ei* directly after the letter *c*
   3. For *long-A-as-in-weigh,* use *ei* at all times
   4. For *long-I-as-in-height,* use *ei* except in *fiery, hieroglyphic* and *hierarchy.*

5. Keep in mind seventeen special exceptions to rules 1 and 2, seven of which are particularly important.

TEST YOURSELF

Decide on the proper combination, *ie* or *ei*, then rewrite the complete word.

1. f—rce _____ (ie)

2. bel—ve _____ (ie)

3. n—ce _____ (ie)

4. rec—ve _____ (ei)

5. c—ling _____ (ei)

6. f—ld _____ (ie)

7. ach—ve _____ (ie)

8. cod—ne _____ (ei)

9. p—ce _____ (ie)

10. financ—r _____ (ie)

11. y—ld _____ (ie)

12. f—nd _____ (ie)

13. conc—ve _____ (ei)

14. p—rce _____ (ie)

15. shr—k _____ (ie)

16. repr—ve _____ (ie)

17. prot—n _____ (ei)

18. br—f _____ (ie)

19. s—ze _____ (ei)

20. l—f _____ (ie)

21. m—n _____ (ie)

22. s—zure _____ (ei)

23. retr—ve _____ (ie)

24. w—rd _____ (ei)

25. sh—ld _____ (ie)

26. sh—k _____ (ei)

27. 1—sure _____ (ei)

28. rel—f _____ (ie)

29. w—r _____ (ei)

30. cash—r _____ (ie)

31. dec—ve _____ (ei)

32. chiffon—r _____ (ie)

33. dec—t _____ (ei)

34. R—d _____ (ei)

35. front—r _____ (ie)

36. f—rcely _____ (ie)

37. —ther _____ (ei)

38. pr—st _____ (ie)

39. rab—s _____ (ie)

40. N—1 _____ (ei)

41. scab—s _____ (ie)

42. caff—ne _____ (ei)

43. chandel—r _____ (ie)

44. K—th _____ (ei)

45. rec—pt _____ (ei)

46. inv—gle _____ (ei)

47. w—ght _____ (ei)

48. r—gn _____ (ei)

49. h—nous _____ (ei)

50. v—n _____ (ei)

51. f—ry _____ (ie)

52. sl—ght _____ (ei)

53. sk—n _____ (ei)

54. —derdown _____ (ei)

55. s—smic _____ (ei)

56. h—roglyphic _____ (ie)

57. h—ght _____ (ei)

58. kal—doscope _____ (ei)

59. st—n _____ (ei)

60. Fahrenh—t _____ (ei)

61. h—rarchy _____ (ie)

62. f—gn _____ (ei)

A Footnote on the Pronunciation of Inveigle

There is, as you probably know, a numerous class of English words which have two current pronunciations. There is the popular, everyday form used by the average man in the streets. And there is also the supposedly "cultivated" form, which has a great attraction for some people who like to consider themselves linguistically sophisticated.

Cases in point are *exquisite, coupon, adult, duty,* and *gratis.* Common, and fully acceptable, pronunciations for these words are *ex-KWIZ-it, KYOO-pon, AD-ult, DOO-tee,* and *GRAT-is;* but there are those speakers who prefer the more scholarly *EX-kwi-zit, KOO-pon, a-DULT, DYOO-tee,* and *GRAY-tis.* And a further case in point is *inveigle.* The scholarly, conservative pronunciation is *in-VEE-g'l,* which throws the word into the exceptional group of those that have a *long-E-as-in-grief* syllable, but which, like *leisure, weird, seize,* etc., nevertheless contains the spelling pattern *ei* not preceded by *c.*

However, for years, the very, very popular pronunciation of *inveigle* has been *in-VAY-g'l,* and is so sanctioned (along with

in-VEE-g'l) by up-to-date dictionaries.   As *in-VAY-g'l*, the word
is no spelling problem — it belongs with all those which contain
a *long-A-as-in-weigh* syllable and are spelled *ei*.

So pronounce *inveigle* however it sounds most comfortable to
you — but spell it only *inveigle*.

9

How to Decide Between *ie* and *ei* in Short Syllables

PROBLEMS
sieve *or* seive?
freind *or* friend?
mischief *or* mischeif?

SOLUTION
You will recall that the problem of *ie* or *ei* in long syllables is solved under the following rules:

1. *Long-E-as-in-grief*, use *ie*:

   ach**ie**ve _____   th**ie**f _____

   n**ie**ce _____   s**ie**ge _____

2. Exceptions to remember are:

   s**ei**ze _____   l**ei**sure _____

   s**ei**zure _____   sh**ei**k _____

   w**ei**rd _____   inv**ei**gle _____

   w**ei**r _____

3. After c, use *ei*:

   re**cei**ve _____   **cei**ling _____

The notable exception is

   finan**cie**r _____

4. *Long-A-as-in-neighbor,* use *ei:*

   freight _____   weight _____

   rein _____   vein _____

5. *Long-I-as-in-height,* use *ei:*

   sleight _____   seismic _____

   stein _____   Fahrenheit _____

6. Exceptions are:

   hierarchy _____   fiery _____

   hieroglyphic _____

All right— so far, so good.

But what if an *ie-ei* combination has a pronunciation other than long *E,* long *A,* or long *I*?

What if the combination has a *short* sound, as in *forfeit* (short *I*), or as in *friend* (short *E*)?

Then we have to be careful.

For in special instances we use *ei.*

But in other instances we use *ie.*

This may at first sound confusing, so let's go slow.

Item: For short syllables, we use *ei* in the *-feit* words:

   counter**feit** _____   sur**feit** _____

   for**feit** _____

Item: *ei* also in the *-eign* words:

   for**eign** _____   sover**eign** _____

   for**eign**er _____   sover**eign**ty _____

Item: And *ei* again in these two words:

   nonpar**eil** _____   h**eif**er _____
   (pronounced *non-pa-RELL)*

Become visually and kinesthetically adjusted to the combination *ei* in *nonpareil,* in *heifer,* and in the *-eit* and *-eign* words — and the problem of *ie* or *ei* in short syllables can be solved instantaneously and automatically —

For all others, without exception, are spelled *ie*.

For example:

handkerch**ie**f _____	anc**ie**nt _____
kerch**ie**f _____	effic**ie**nt _____
misch**ie**f _____	omnisc**ie**nce _____
misch**ie**vous _____	consc**ie**nce _____
effic**ie**nt _____	quot**ie**nt _____
defic**ie**nt _____	trans**ie**nt _____
suffic**ie**nt _____	s**ie**ve _____
profic**ie**nt _____	fr**ie**nd _____
pat**ie**nt _____	etc.

Nothing, I think you'll agree, can be less confusing. The basic principle is perfectly clear:

Point 12

In short syllables, the general combination is *ie*. However, in *nonpareil* and *heifer*, and in *-eit* and *-eign* words, the correct pattern is *ei*.

TEST YOURSELF

Decide on the missing combination (*ie* or *ei*), then rewrite the complete word.

1. forf—t _____ (ei)

2. for—gn _____ (ei)

3. counterf—t _____ (ei)

4. sover—gn _____ (ei)

5. surf—t _____ (ei)

6. s—ve _____ (ie)

7. handkerch—f _____ (ie)

8. nonpar—l _____ (ei)

9. misch—vous _____ (ie)

10. anc—nt _____ (ie)

11. h—fer _____ (ei)

12. kerch—f _____ (ie)

13. fr—nd _____ (ie)

14. trans—nt _____ (ie)

15. misch—f _____ (ie)

16. pat—nt _____ (ie)

17. profic—nt _____ (ie)

18. consc—nce _____ (ie)

A Footnote on Nonpareil and Friend

Students of the French language have no difficulty spelling *nonpareil* — this word is a direct import from the Gallic tongue and, as so often happens, retains its foreign spelling even though the pronunciation has been completely Anglicized. (We say *non-pa-RELL*, quite different from what the French say.)

Pareil is the French term for *equal; non* is of course a sign of the negative. So in French, as also in English, the word means *having no equal, in a class by itself.* It is not in particularly common use, except, as it happens, as the name of a type of candy with a chocolate bottom and little white sugar dots. And there is no reason why you should have to be able to spell it, unless you have a passion for feeling completely self-assured that you know the correct pattern of any word that has even the remotest chance of being offered you; or unless, of course, you are preparing for the spelling section of a Civil Service test, on which the most amazing words always occur.

Friend, however, is in a very different category — it is a most common word in everyday use, and anyone beyond the fourth grade of grammar school is expected to be able to spell it correctly.

Yet, for some strange and unexplainable reason, many otherwise educated people are stumped by this simple word, never quite sure whether to write *ie* or *ei* — and often, unhappily, finally deciding on *ei*. If the word was ever a problem to you, it need no longer be so; you know that short syllables are usually spelled *ie* except in the *-eign* and *-eit* groups and in the two special words *heifer* and *nonpareil*.

10

(*Fifth Day*)

First Review

Let us stop for a moment, now, so you can catch your breath.
Let us review all you've learned thus far.
Let us wrap all the facts and figures into a neat package.

We have thoroughly covered the following basic principles:

Supersede is the only word in the English language ending in -*sede*.

      supers**ede** _____

Three, and only three, words end in -*ceed*, keyed to the phrase *Full Speed Ahead*.

    suc**ceed** _____ ex**ceed** _____

    pro**ceed** _____

All other "seed" words end in -*cede*.

    ac**cede** _____ pre**cede** _____

    se**cede** _____ re**cede** _____

                 etc.

Procedure and *procedural*, forms of one of the three "speed" words, do not contain a double *e*.

    proc**e**dure _____ proc**e**dural _____

Most words end in -*ize* in preference to -*ise* or -*yze*.

    apolog**ize** _____ hypnot**ize** _____

                 etc.

Two common words end in -*yze*.

   ana**lyze** _____ para**lyze** _____

Thirty-six common words end in -*ise*.

   adv**ise** _____ surpr**ise** _____

   dev**ise** _____ surm**ise** _____

                    etc.

Miss- occurs at the beginning of a word if the root starts with *s*.

   mi**ss**hapen _____ mi**ss**pelling _____

                    etc.

Diss- occurs at the beginning of a word if the root starts with *s*.

   di**ss**atisfy _____ di**ss**imilar _____

                    etc.

Dis- occurs at the beginning of a word if the root does not start with *s*.

   di**sapp**ear _____ di**sapp**rove _____

   di**sapp**oint _____ di**s**concert _____

                    etc.

Dys- occurs at the beginning of two words:

   dyspeptic _____ **dys**entery _____

For the long *E* sound, *ie* is the usual combination:

   n**ie**ce _____ f**ie**ld _____

   ach**ie**ve _____ p**ie**ce _____

                    etc.

Seven important words are exceptions to the *ie* rule:

   s**ei**ze _____ w**ei**rd _____

   s**ei**zure _____ w**ei**r _____

l**ei**sure _____   inv**ei**gle _____

sh**ei**k _____

However, directly after the letter c, *ei* is used.

re**cei**ve _____   **cei**ling _____

With one glaring exception:

fonan**cier** _____

In syllables with a *long A* pronunciation, *ei* is required.

n**eigh** _____   v**eil** _____

In syllables with a *long I* pronunciation, *ei* is again required.

h**eigh**t _____   st**ein** _____

Three exceptions are:

f**ie**ry _____   h**ie**rarchy _____

h**ie**roglyphic _____

In syllables with a *short* pronunciation, *ei* is required in the *-eit* and *-eign* words:

counterf**eit** _____   for**eign** _____

etc.

And also in two special words:

nonpar**eil** _____   h**ei**fer _____

For all other words with *short* syllables *ie* is correct.

s**ie**ve _____   anc**ie**nt _____

fr**ie**nd _____   consc**ie**nce _____

etc.

FIRST REVIEW TEST

I. Check the correct pattern.
    1. (a) supercede, (b) supersede   (b)
    2. (a) procede,   (b) proceed   (b)

3. (a) excede,   (b) exceed   (b)
4. (a) precede,   (b) preceed   (a)
5. (a) conceed,   (b) concede   (b)
6. (a) procedure, (b) proceedure   (a)

II. Attach the correct ending, choosing between *-ise, -ize,* and *-yze,* rewriting the complete word.

1. paral— _____ (yze)

2. anal— _____ (yze)

3. advert— _____ (ise)

4. appr— _____ (ise)

5. surm— _____ (ise)

6. superv— _____ (ise)

7. improv— _____ (ise)

8. comprom— _____ (ise)

9. surpr— _____ (ise)

10. compr— _____ (ise)

11. apolog— _____ (ize)

12. character— _____ (ize)

13. memor— _____ (ize)

14. ostrac— _____ (ize)

III. Begin each word with *mis-* or *miss-,* as required, rewriting the complete word.

1. —pelling _____ (miss)

2. —tatement _____ (miss)

3. —tep _____ (miss)

4. —pent _____ (miss)

5. —construe _____ (mis)

6. —hap _____ (mis)

7. —hapen _____ (miss)

8. —cellaneous _____ (mis)

IV. Begin each with word *dis-*, *diss-*, or *dys-*, as required, rewriting the complete word.

1. —appear _____ (dis)

2. —appoint _____ (dis)

3. —approve _____ (dis)

4. —peptic _____ (dys)

5. —entery _____ (dys)

6. —atisfy _____ (diss)

7. —ertation _____ (diss)

8. —ever _____ (diss)

9. —imilar _____ (diss)

10. —ociate _____ (diss)

11. —olute _____ (diss)

12. —uade _____ (diss)

13. —yllable _____ (diss)

14. —agree _____ (dis)

15. —allow _____ (dis)

V. Fill in *ie* or *ei*, as required, rewriting the complete word.

1. rec—ve _____ (ei)

2. dec—t _____ (ei)

3. bel—ve _____ (ie)

4. f—ld _____ (ie)

5. n—ce _____ (ie)

6. y—ld _____ (ie)

7. s—zure _____ (ei)

8. financ—r _____ (ie)

9. sh—k _____ (ei)

10. w—rd _____ (ei)

11. w—r _____ (ei)

12. l—sure _____ (ei)

13. chandel—r _____ (ie)

14. w—gh _____ (ei)

15. h—nous _____ (ei)

16. inv—gle _____ (ei)

17. r—gn _____ (ei)

18. inv—gh _____ (ei)

19. h—ght _____ (ei)

20. st—n _____ (ei)

21. f—ry _____ (ie)

22. counterf—t _____ (ei)

23. forf—t _____ (ei)

24. sover—gn _____ (ei)

25. misch—f _____ (ie)

26. s—ve _____ (ie)

27. fr—nd _____ (ie)

28. consc—nce _____ (ie)

11

When to Drop a Final e

PROBLEMS
desireable *or* desirable?
stoney *or* stony?
likeable *or* likable?

SOLUTION
There is, then, a certain rudimentary logic to English spelling.

No one in his right mind would call our system of spelling "completely logical," "eminently logical," or even "fairly logical"; on the other hand, it is somewhat prejudiced to label it "thoroughly illogical" or "absolutely fantastic." There are some strong threads of logic running through it, with many illogical threads interspersed — and with a little practice and understanding it is possible, as I hope you have seen, to come to terms with spelling, to declare a kind of armed truce, even to arrive quite close to mastery.

One of your potent allies in the conquest and mastery of English spelling is a basic human ability — the ability to become used to something if it is repeated often enough.

Take, for example, the word *come*. It would be far more logical to spell it *cum* or even *kum*, but no normal human being who has progressed beyond the fourth grade in school is ever tempted to spell it in that sane and sensible way. (How sensible *cum* would be may be judged from the fact that *come* is derived from the Anglo-Saxon word *cuman*.) Indeed, *cum* or *kum* appearing in a page of print would at once arrest the eye. Sane and sensible as it may be, it looks ridiculous — because, through repetition and habit, we are completely adjusted to seeing and writing *come*.

Similarly, no one ever misspells *move*, *like*, *love*, *prove*, *hate*, *make*, *wave*, *give*, *change*, *desire*, etc. In each case we use the final *e*, expect to see it in print, and require it to pronounce the word correctly.

But some of us become overly attached to that final -*e*, and through either accident or ignorance keep it in a word even when it no longer belongs there. In the writing of a poor speller, it is not uncommon to find errors like:

comeing	moveing	likeing
loveable	proveable	hateing
makeing	waveing	giveing
changeing	arriveal	desireable
	etc.	

If every one of these spellings looks peculiar to you, this is not the type of error you make. And you can, with a little thought, see the basic principle that operates:

Point 13
When a word ends in *e* —

> (*prove, stone, value, desire*)

Drop that *e* —

> (*prov-, ston-, valu-, desir-*)

Before adding a suffix that begins with a vowel.

> (*prov-ing, ston-y,*[1] *valu-able, desir-able*, etc.)

Nothing very unusual here — an important tendency in English is the avoidance of two vowels where one will do.

So the following spellings are correct:

(come)	coming
(move)	moving, movable
(like)	liking, likable[2]
(love)	loving, lovable[2]
(prove)	proving, provable
(hate)	hating

[1]Many people think we have only five vowels, *a, e, i, o, u;* but *y* is almost always a vowel if it is not the first letter of a word.

[2]*Likeable* and *loveable* are not wrong; but *likable* and *lovable* are the preferred spellings.

(make)	making
(value)	valuable
(wave)	waving
(give)	giving
(stone)	stony
(change)	changing
(sale)	salable
(bone)	bony
(desire)	desirable, desiring
(arrive)	arriving, arrival
(argue)	arguing, argued

So you know that it is normal and proper to drop a final e before adding a vowel ending.

What if you add a consonant ending, such as *-ment, -ful,* or *-ness?*

Point 14

Final e is *retained* when you add a suffix beginning with a consonant.

For example:

WORD	CONSONANT	VOWEL
state	statement	stat/ing
refine	refinement	refin/ing
sure	sureness	sur/est
grace	graceful	grac/ing
care	careful	car/ing
encourage	encouragement	encourag/ing
waste	wasteful	wast/ing
true	trueness	tru/er
vague	vaguely	vagu/er

And that's all there is to it — drop final e before a vowel, keep it before a consonant.

Such a simple principle, you probably suspect, is subject to exceptions.

What these exceptions are, and how they operate, we will consider in subsequent chapters.

TEST YOURSELF

Rewrite each word, adding the indicated suffix.

1. like + *able* _____ (likable)

2. love + *able* _____ (lovable)

3. prove + *able* _____ (provable)

4. give + *ing* _____ (giving)

5. bone + y _____ (bony)

6. stone + y _____ (stony)

7. argue + *ing* _____ (arguing)

8. value + *able* _____ (valuable)

9. care + *ful* _____ (careful)

10. true + *ness* _____ (trueness)

PRETEST

1. exhi**ll**arate, exhi**ll**erate, *or* exhilarate?
2. vi**c**ious *or* vis**c**ious?
3. re**d**iculous *or* ri**d**iculous?
4. **des**cription *or* **dis**cription?
5. rep**e**tition *or* rep**i**tition?
6. re**cc**omend *or* re**c**ommend?
7. b**ui**sness *or* b**u**siness?
8. holiday *or* ho**ll**iday?
9. ab**sc**ence *or* ab**s**ence?
10. di**s**pair *or* de**s**pair?

MNEMONICS

Understanding is a matter of seeing relationships.

As you begin to understand English spelling, you will see more and more relationships — between various words, between the letters of words, between the pattern of a word's spelling and the Latin or Greek root from which the word derives.

You are now beginning to understand the reasons behind the correct spellings of English words.

You know that the reason behind the ending in *supersede* is its Latin derivation, *sedeo*, to sit.

You know that the reason behind the endings in *accede, precede, secede,* etc., is their Latin derivation *cedo*, to go.

You know that the reason behind the double *s* in *misspelling, misshapen, dissyllable, dissuade,* etc., is that the prefix *mis-* or *dis-* is attached to a root starting with an *s*.

You know that *dissipate* is spelled as it is because the prefix *dis-* is tacked on to the root *sip*, to throw.

You can now also begin to think of words in groups. *Superintendent, persistent, insistent,* and *dependent* belong in one group.

Anoint and *inoculate* belong in another. *Succeed, proceed,* and *exceed* belong in a third. *Paralyze* and *analyze* belong in a fourth. *Dysentery* and *dyspeptic* belong in a fifth. And so on.

The sharpening of your sense of relationships will help you to build accurate and automatic habits of good spelling, will increase your confidence in your ability to choose the correct pattern under all circumstances.

Our interest in this chapter will again be focused on relationships, in this case the relationship between a difficult form of a word and an easily spelled form of the same word.

Let me illustrate.

1. HIL**A**RIOUS, *very merry, noisily gay,* is rarely misspelled even by the most confused and inefficient of spellers, for the pattern exactly follows the sound. Yet another form of the same word, EXHIL**A**RATE, is almost consistently misspelled by even the most literate and sophisticated of writers. If you think of the easily spelled HIL**A**RIOUS, and note the single *l* followed by *a,* you will have no difficulty spelling

EXHIL**A**RATE _____

2. V**ICE** is the easily spelled form of V**ICI**OUS — see this relationship and you'll feel no temptation to misspell the word.

V**ICI**OUS _____

3. R**I**DICULE, spelled exactly as it sounds, rarely causes trouble; keep this form in mind when you write R**I**DICULOUS, which is not necessarily spelled exactly as it sounds — some speakers make the first syllable identical to that in *receive.*

R**I**DICULOUS _____

4. For some unexplainable reason, practically no one misspells D**E**SCRIBE — but approximately 20 per cent of any random group of literate people misspell the noun form D**E**SCRIPTION. Note the identical first syllable on both forms:

D**E**SCRIPTION _____

5. REP**E**AT, like D**E**SCRIBE, is practically never misspelled — but its related form, REP**E**TITION, frequently is. Note that in REP**E**AT the *p* is followed by *e* — as also in REP**E**TITION. (The

same principle works in COMPETE — COMPETITION; an e after the *p* in each case.)

REPETITION _____

6. COMMEND is rarely misspelled — keep the word in mind when you add the prefix *re-*, *again*. So to COMMEND *again* is to

RECOMMEND _____

7. BUSY has never, to my knowledge, stumped a speller who has advanced beyond the third grade of elementary school — but its related form BUSINESS (BUSY + NESS) takes its toll of approximately 10 per cent of literate people.

BUSINESS _____

8. HOLIDAY has one *l* — it is a HOLY DAY (originally, holidays were all of religious significance), and the *y* changes to *i* as it does when BUSYNESS becomes BUSINESS.

HOLIDAY _____

9. The obviously related form ABSENT has no c — hence ABSENCE, not *abscence*.

ABSENCE _____

10. DESPAIR does not follow the pronunciation — but its allied form DESPERATE does, at least in the first syllable; and from DESPERATE we have the key to the first syllable *des-* rather than *dis-*.

DESPERATE _____

MNEMONICS CHART

Note, then, what we are doing.

As a general mnemonic, we are taking a difficult-to-spell form of a word and relating it to an easily spelled form — and the easy form steers us away from any error in the pattern of the confusing form.

	Correct Pattern	Mnemonic
1. exhilarate	_____	hilarious
2. vicious	_____	vice

	Correct Pattern	*Mnemonic*
3. ridiculous	_____	ridicule
4. description	_____	describe
5. repetition	_____	repeat
6. recommend	_____	commend
7. business	_____	busy
8. holiday	_____	holy
9. absence	_____	absent
10. despair	_____	desperate

TEST YOURSELF

I. Check the correct pattern.

1. (a) reccomend, (b) recommend   (b)
2. (a) description, (b) discription   (a)
3. (a) buisness, (b) business   (b)
4. (a) holiday, (b) holliday   (a)
5. (a) abscence, (b) absence   (b)
6. (a) dispairing, (b) despairing   (b)
7. (a) viscious, (b) vicious   (b)
8. (a) exhillerate, (b) exhillarate, (c) exhilarate   (c)
9. (a) ridiculous, (b) rediculous   (a)
10. (a) repetition, (b) repitition   (a)

II. Recall the mnemonic for each word.

1. exhilarate	_____	(hilarious)
2. vicious	_____	(vice)
3. ridiculous	_____	(ridicule)
4. description	_____	(describe)
5. repetition	_____	(repeat)
6. recommend	_____	(commend)
7. business	_____	(busy)
8. absence	_____	(absent)

9. holiday _____ (holy)

10. despair _____ (desperate)

11. occurrence _____ (current event)

12. superintendent _____ (rent)

13. inoculate _____ (inject)

14. indispensable _____ (able worker)

15. dependable _____ (able worker)

16. siege _____ (city)

17. seize _____ (neck)

18. battalion _____ (battle)

19. parallel _____ (all tracks)

20. fricassee _____ (casserole)

21. persistent _____ (rent)

22. insistent _____ (rent)

23. dependent _____ (rent)

24. embarrassed _____ (two robbers, Sing Sing, ass)

25. anoint _____ (an oil)

III. Decide on the missing crucial letters, then rewrite the complete word.

1. emba—a—ed _____ (rr,ss)

2. ba—a—ion _____ (tt,l)

3. s—ge _____ (ie)

4. s—ze _____ (ei)

5. depend—ble _____ (a)

6. occu—nce _____ (rre)

7. d—spair _____ (e)

8. exhi—rate _____ (la)

9. abs—nce _____ (e)

10. rep—tition _____ (e)

11. b—ness _____ (usi)

12. d—scription _____ (e)

13. superintend—nt _____ (e)

14. a—oint _____ (n)

15. para—e— _____ (ll,l)

16. i—o—ulate _____ (n,c)

17. indispens—ble _____ (a)

18. fri—a—ee _____ (c,ss)

19. persist—nt _____ (e)

20. r—diculous _____ (i)

21. ho—iday _____ (l)

22. depend—nt _____ (e)

23. re—o—end _____ (c,mm)

24. insist—nt _____ (e)

25. vi—ious _____ (c)

A Footnote on Kinesthetic Training

In this chapter you have had a chance to write each new word at least four times — in addition you have written once again, in its correct pattern, every word from all previous mnemonics chapters.

This is kinesthetic practice of the most valuable kind — it is meaningful, combined with thinking, controlled by intellectual processes.

You have doubtless heard the story of the fourth-grade youngster who had developed the quaint but socially unacceptable habit of saying *I have went.* His teacher, somewhat confused about the principles of effective learning, decided that kinesthetic practice would cure her charge of his unfortunate lapse from correct usage.

So she instructed him to stay after school and write one thousand times on the blackboards which surrounded the classroom the sentence *I have gone*. She warned the child that when she returned in the morning she would make a careful count, and left the school with the warm feeling that she finally had found a way to lick the problem.

The next morning she counted a full thousand carefully written *I have gone's;* and found on her desk this significant note: "Dear teacher, I have done the work and I have went home."

Which proves that *meaningless* kinesthetic practice is a waste of time. Mere repetition will result in muscle fatigue, not in actual learning. But when you train your muscles to respond accurately to a practical situation, when you keep changing the situation while still calling for the same muscular response, then eventually your muscles can, in a sense, do their own thinking and react automatically and correctly.

Many of the activities you have learned in meaningful situations, and have repeated under changing stimuli, are now part of your "muscle thinking." If you drive a car, you make automatic muscular responses to the stimuli of familiar road conditions — the changing traffic lights, the actions of the car ahead, the erratic behavior of the death-defying pedestrians. When you buy in a familiar supermarket, you walk automatically to the proper shelves in response to the demands of your shopping list. In all these and similar cases you have, through meaningful practice, developed automatic and accurate muscular responses; you have driven your learning to lower-than-conscious levels and no longer need make conscious mental decisions.

And this is the result you are aiming for in your spelling — by writing a word a calculated number of times in response to changing situations you are letting your muscles as well as your mind become accustomed to the desirable patterns — eventually old and undesirable patterns will fade and be lost and the new, correct patterns will be as much an integral part of your "muscle thinking" as the way you dress in the morning, drive your car, comb your hair, or do any other work at which you have developed skill.

So resist the temptation to merely *read* these chapters — fill every blank with the required words in your own handwriting, keep teaching your muscles to react accurately. From kinesthetic practice will come the self-assurance in spelling that you are working for.

12

When to Keep the e After c

PROBLEMS
noticeable *or* noticable?
serviceable *or* servicable?

SOLUTION
C is a tricky letter.
And so it often makes for tricky and problem spellings.
There is a so-called "soft" and a so-called "hard" c.
Soft c has the sound of *s* in *sit*. Examples of soft c are:

city	notice
civil	mercy
pace	cylinder

Notice, then, that before the vowels *e, i,* and *y,*[1] c is usually soft. *e, i,* and *y* are therefore called "softening" vowels.
Hard c has the sound of *k* in *Kate*. Examples of hard c are:

cavern	panic
cost	closet
current	

Notice, then, that before the vowels *a, o,* and *u,* c is usually hard. *A, o* and *u* are therefore called "hardening" vowels. C is also hard;

      1. as the *final* letter in a word; and
      2. before a consonant.

Keep these facts in mind, understand them thoroughly, and you will automatically solve a number of vexing problems.

[1] You will recall that we consider *y* the sixth vowel.

84

Point 15

C *is usually soft*
— before e *(cent)*
— before i *(cinch)*
— before y *(cycle)*
(e, i, and y are "softening" vowels)

Point 16

C *is usually hard*
— before a *(car)*
— before o *(come)*
— before u *(cur)*
(a, o, and u are "hardening" vowels)
— as a final letter *(public)*
— before consonants *(cry)*

The Vexing Problems
Which is correct.

noticable *or* noticeable?
servicable *or* serviceable?
embracable *or* embraceable?

We can now solve this type of problem easily and clearly.

Take the word *notice*. The c is soft (like s), coming before the softening vowel e.

Now take the misspelling *noticable*. Here, the c would be hard (like k), coming before the hardening vowel a. If the c were hard, the word would be pronounced *NO-ti-ka-b'l*.

But of course the word is *not* pronounced *NO-ti-ka-b'l*. As everyone knows, it is pronounced *NO-ti-sa-b'l*.

So —

To keep the c soft, we must separate it from the hardening vowel a.

We separate the c from the hardening vowel a by retaining the softening final e of *notice*. Correct spelling:

noticeable _____

Take the word *service*. The c is soft (like s), coming before the softening vowel e.

Now take the misspelling *servicable*. Here, the c would be hard (like *k*), coming before the hardening vowel *a*. If the c were hard, the word would be pronounced *SER-vik-a-b'l*. Again, as everyone knows, the correct pronunciation is not *SER-vik-a-b'l*, but *SER-vi-sa-b'l*.

So —

To keep the c soft, we must separate it from the hardening vowel *a*.

As in the case of *noticeable*, we separate the c from the hardening vowel *a* by retaining the softening final *e*. Correct spelling:

servi**cea**ble _____

Note these words which contain a soft c.

embrace	trace	peace
lace	service	notice
replace	bounce	pronounce
	enforce	

If we wish to add *-able*, a suffix which starts with the hardening vowel *a*, we must retain the softening final *e* in each word.

embra**cea**ble _____   boun**cea**ble _____

la**cea**ble _____   pea**cea**ble _____

repla**cea**ble _____   noti**cea**ble _____

irrepla**cea**ble _____   pronoun**cea**ble _____

tra**cea**ble _____   enfor**cea**ble _____

servi**cea**ble _____

(*Tracing, servicing*, etc., offer no problem — *i*, like *e*, is a softening vowel.)

Understand why the extra *e* is required, commit these words to visual memory, and you can eliminate another tricky and confusing problem in English spelling.

TEST YOURSELF

Add the suffix *-able* to the following verbs, rewriting the complete word. Decide, in each case, whether or not to retain the softening *e*.

1. enforce _____ (enforceable)

2. pronounce _____ (pronounceable)

3. embrace _____ (embraceable)

4. lace _____ (laceable)

5. seize _____ (seizable)

6. notice _____ (noticeable)

7. dispense _____ (dispensable)

8. peace _____ (peaceable)

9. replace _____ (replaceable)

10. use _____ (usable)

11. (ir)replace _____ (irreplaceable)

12. bounce _____ (bounceable)

13. believe _____ (believable)

14. service _____ (serviceable)

15. pleasure _____ (pleasurable)

16. trace _____ (traceable)

17. value _____ (valuable)

18. blame _____ (blamable)

13

When to Use a *k* After c

PROBLEMS
panic**y** *or* panic**ky**?
froli**c**ing *or* froli**ck**ing?
traffi**cer** *or* traffi**cker**?

SOLUTION
Now let us look at the other side of the coin — hard c's which must be kept hard. When c is the final letter of a word, it is, as you know, pronounced like *k*.

For example:

zinc	panic
colic	picnic
frolic	traffic
physic	bivouac
mimic	shellac

Take the verb to *picnic*.

Suppose you wish to add the suffix *-er*, to denote *one who picnics*.

Your immediate temptation might be, in all innocence and directness, to write: *picnicer.*

But hold on!

c *before* e *is soft, as you have learned.*

The word would then be pronounced *PIK-niss-er*, obviously absurd.

We must do something to keep the c hard (like *k*) before a softening vowel (e).

So we do the obvious thing — we slip in a *k*.

And we get:

picni**cker** _____

88

This may look awkward and unfamiliar — maybe unpleasant.

You will get used to it.

Other forms of *picnic* are spelled similarly, even though they may look similarly awkward, unfamiliar, and unpleasant.

picnicking _____   picnicked _____

And the same principle operates in other final -c words:

zincking _____   frolicker _____

colicky _____   physicking _____

frolicking _____   panicked _____

frolicked _____   shellacked _____

mimicked _____   trafficked _____

mimicking _____   trafficking _____

panicky _____   bivouacking _____

trafficker _____   bivouacked _____

etc.

Point 17

When a word ends in c, like *picnic, frolic, panic,* or *traffic* —

And you wish to add *-ed, -er, -ing,* or *-y* (all softening vowels) —

First insert the letter *k* before these vowels —

And you will keep the pronunciation sane and sensible.

So watch your c's

To keep them soft before *-able*, retain the softening *e*.

To keep them hard before *-ed, -er, -ing,* or *-y*, insert *k*.

And let your visual memory do the rest.

TEST YOURSELF

Add the required suffixes to each of the following words, rewriting the complete word.

I. Add *-ing* to:

1. frolic _____   (frolicking)

2. panic _____   (panicking)

   3. picnic _____   (picni**ck**ing)

   4. traffic _____   (traffi**ck**ing)

   5. zinc _____   (zin**ck**ing)

   6. physic _____   (physi**ck**ing)

   7. politic _____   (politi**ck**ing)

   8. bivouac _____   (bivoua**ck**ing)

   9. mimic _____   (mimi**ck**ing)

  10. shellac _____   (shella**ck**ing)

II. Add -*er* to:

   1. picnic _____   (picni**ck**er)

   2. traffic _____   (traffi**ck**er)

   3. bivouac _____   (bivoua**ck**er)

   4. frolic _____   (froli**ck**er)

III. Add -*ed* to:

   1. picnic _____   (picni**ck**ed)

   2. frolic _____   (froli**ck**ed)

   3. panic _____   (pani**ck**ed)

   4. traffic _____   (traffi**ck**ed)

   5. zinc _____   (zin**ck**ed)

   6. physic _____   (physi**ck**ed)

   7. politic _____   (politi**ck**ed)

   8. bivouac _____   (bivoua**ck**ed)

   9. mimic _____   (mimi**ck**ed)

  10. shellac _____   (shella**ck**ed)

A Footnote on Zinc, Physic, Politic, and Bivouac

The words discussed in this chapter are all in common use with the exception of *bivouac,* and of *physic, politic,* and *zinc* as verbs.

A *bivouac* is a camp outdoors without tents, hence a kind of temporary shelter. The word is often heard in reference to military maneuvers, as when an army is *bivouacking* before battle, etc.

Physic, politic, and *zinc* are everyday words as nouns — but they are occasionally also used as verbs, as when we say that a mother believes in *physicking* her child at the first sign of a cold (that is, she pours great quantities of Ex-Lax, milk of magnesia, and castor oil into the unhappy youngster); or as when we say that the senator is *politicking* up and down the state (that is, repairing the political fences, as the handy cliché puts it, or making speeches that ask for re-election); or, finally, as when we say that we are in the process of *zincking* an object (that is, putting on a coat of *zinc*).

These verbs are picturesque usages and are gradually becoming more prevalent in speech and writing. Use them whenever you're so minded — and don't forget the very necessary *k* that keeps the c hard.

14

When to Keep the e After g

PROBLEMS

changeable *or* changable?
judgement *or* judgment?
mortgageor *or* mortgagor?

SOLUTION

You will recall that we considered c a tricky letter — because its pronunciation could be either "soft" or "hard."

Equally tricky is *g* — because it, too, can be either "soft" or "hard," and for the same reasons that operate in respect to the letter *c*.

Soft *g* has the sound of *j* in *just:*

advantage	spongy	judgment
change	gypsy	acknowledgment
changing	gin	

Notice, then, that *g*, like *c*, is soft before the softening vowels *e*, *i*, and *y;* and also when preceded by *d*.

Hard *g* has the sound of *g* in *glad:*

gas	gun	pig
gone	grin	ugly

Notice, then, that *g*, again like *c*, is hard before the hardening vowels *a*, *o*, and *u;* as the final letter in a word; and before a consonant.

Keep these facts in mind, understand them thoroughly, and you will again, as with the letter c, automatically solve a number of vexing problems.

92

Point 18
 g is usually soft
  — before *e (gem)*
  — before *i (gin)*
  — before *y (gymnasium)*
 (*e, i,* and *y* are softening vowels)
 (Some short Anglo-Saxon words are obvious exceptions, such as *get, gift,* etc., but they won't trouble you.)
  — after *d (judgment)*

Point 19
 g is usually hard
  — before *a (gadget)*
  — before *o (got)*
  — before *u (guest, intrigue)*
 (*a, o,* and *u* are hardening vowels)
  — as a final letter *(slag, rug)*
  — before consonants *(green, glib)*

The Vexing Problems
 Which is correct:

> change**able** or chang**able**?
> manage**able** or managable?
> advantag**eous** or advantagous?
> abridg**ement** or abridgment?

We can now solve this type of problem quickly and successfully.
Take the word *charge.* The *g* is soft (pronounced like *j*).
We wish to add the suffix *-able.*
But *a* is a hardening vowel.
So we must keep the softening *e* between the *g* and the *a.*
Thus:

> char**gea**ble _____

Similarly:

chan**gea**ble _____	wa**gea**ble _____
marria**gea**ble _____	salva**gea**ble _____
mortga**gea**ble _____	enga**gea**ble _____
mana**gea**ble _____	disenga**gea**ble _____

o, like *a*, is a hardening vowel. If *g* must be pronounced soft before the suffix *-ous*, again we must keep the softening *e*. Thus:

advanta**geous** _____   coura**geous** _____

disadvanta**geous** _____   outra**geous** _____

                                         gor**geous** _____

(This accounts for the strange spelling *George*, to differentiate it in pronunciation from *gorge*.)

Or take *judge, lodge, abridge, acknowledge*.
In each case the *g* is soft, both because of the softening vowel *e* and the preceding *d*.
Now *g* is usually hard before a consonant, as in *segment, ugly,* etc.

Nevertheless —

When we add *-ment* for the purpose of forming nouns from *judge, lodge, abridge,* and *acknowledge*, we eliminate the final *e*, relying on the preceding *d* to keep the *g* soft.
Thus (and these are the preferable spellings):

jud**gment** _____   abrid**gment** _____

lod**gment** _____   acknowled**gment** _____

(On the other hand, words like *disparage, encourage, discourage, enrage, engage,* do not contain a softening *d* — hence the *e* is retained before *-ment: disparagement, encouragement, discouragement, enragement, engagement,* etc. In fact, as you know, final *e* is regularly retained before *-ment* or any suffix beginning with a consonant.)
No exceptions to these principles?
Yes, there are two important types of exceptions to keep in mind.

Point 20

1. Despite the fact that *g* is usually hard before *o, mortgagor* (pronounced *MOR-ga-jer*) does not contain a softening *e*.

                mortga**gor** _____

2. Although a preceding *d* keeps *g* soft in words like *acknowledgeable, bridgeable,* etc., we keep the softening *e* nevertheless, thus protecting the *g* both fore and aft.

acknowled**geable** _____ knowled**geable** _____

brid**geable** _____ abrid**geable** _____

Let me recapitulate briefly:

1. For soft *g*, retain the *e* before *-able* or *-ous:*

mana**geable** _____ outra**geous** _____

gor**geous** _____ chan**geable** _____

2. After *dg*, preferably omit *e* before *-ment:*

ju**dgment** _____ acknowle**dgment** _____

3. Bear in mind the exceptions:

mortga**gor** _____ acknowle**dgeable** _____

knowle**dgeable** _____ bri**dgeable** _____

TEST YOURSELF

I. Rewrite the following words with an *-able* ending.

1. charge _____ (chargeable)

2. believe _____ (believable)

3. marriage _____ (marriageable)

4. bridge _____ (bridgeable)

5. acknowledge _____ (acknowledgeable)

6. change _____ (changeable)

7. pleasure _____ (pleasurable)

8. enrage _____ (enrageable)

9. manage _____ (manageable)

10. salvage _____ (salvageable)

11. engage _____ (engageable)

12. disengage _____ (disenga**gea**ble)

13. value _____ (val**ua**ble)

14. mortgage _____ (mortga**gea**ble)

II. Rewrite the following words with an *-ous* ending.

1. advantage _____ (advanta**geous**)

2. disadvantage _____ (disadvanta**geous**)

3. courage _____ (coura**geous**)

4. outrage _____ (outra**geous**)

5. (gorge) _____ (gor**geous**)

III. Rewrite the following words with an *-ment* ending, using the preferable spelling.

1. judge _____ (jud**gment**)

2. advertise _____ (advertisement)

3. lodge _____ (lod**gment**)

4. abridge _____ (abrid**gment**)

5. disable _____ (disablement)

6. acknowledge _____ (acknowled**gment**)

7. disparage _____ (dispara**gement**)

8. encourage _____ (encoura**gement**)

9. discourage _____ (discoura**gement**)

10. engage _____ (enga**gement**)

11. disengage _____ (disenga**gement**) ·

IV. Rewrite the following word with an *-or* ending.

1. mortgage _____ (mortga**gor**)

PRETEST
1. alright *or* all right?
2. baloon *or* balloon?
3. pursuit *or* persuit?
4. sherrif *or* sheriff?
5. catagory *or* category?

MNEMONICS

1. (alright *or* all right?)

It is often said that this word has two spellings — the one most people use, and the correct one.

It is certainly logical enough to misspell the word in the pattern *alright* — it fits perfectly into the group of similar words: *already, altogether, also, almighty*, etc. But A**LL** RIGHT is the lone wolf, the rebel, the nonconformist in this group. It is acceptable only in the two-word, two-l pattern.

Of all the words in the English language (over 600,000 by last count) A**LL** RIGHT is without question the most frequently misspelled. Do not be surprised if you see it written *alright* occasionally in magazines and newspapers, frequently in letters written by otherwise civilized and erudite correspondents.

How can you remember its proper and accepted pattern? The mnemonic is simple — link it with its opposite, A**LL** WRONG. A**LL** RIGHT follows essentially the same form — two words, two l's.

> *Correct Spelling:* all right _____
>
> *Mnemonic:*   all wrong

2. (baloon *or* balloon?)

A BA**LL**OON, as even a young child knows, is usually a round object, a kind of BA**LL**. By linking BA**LL**OON to BA**LL**, you will automatically avoid the popular misspelling.

Correct Spelling: balloon _____

Mnemonic: ba**ll**

3. (p**u**rsuit *or* p**e**rsuit?)

Get this picture: A thief snatches your P**U**RSE — you tear after him in hot P**U**RSUIT.

Correct Spelling: p**u**rsuit _____

Mnemonic: p**u**rse

4. (she**rr**i**f** *or* she**r**i**ff**?)

The problem in this word is the number of **r**'s and **f**'s. Keep in mind that a SHE**R**I**FF**'S duty is to protect respectable people against the **R**I**FF**-**R**A**FF** — hence one **r**, two **f**'s.

Correct Spelling: she**r**i**ff** _____

Mnemonic: **r**i**ff**-**r**a**ff**

(TA**R**I**FF**, by the way, follows the same pattern as SHE**R**I**FF** — one **r**, two **f**'s.)

5. (cat**a**gory *or* cat**e**gory?)

The crucial letter in this word, as you can see, is the vowel following the *t* — is it an *a* or an *e*? One useful type of mnemonic is an easily spelled synonym of the problem word, a synonym that contains the correct crucial letters — in this case S**E**CTION, which is one of the synonyms of CAT**E**GORY, and which highlights the *e*.

Correct Spelling: cat**e**gory _____

Mnemonic: s**e**ction

MNEMONICS CHART

Correct Pattern		*Mnemonic*
a**ll** right	_____	a**ll** wrong
ba**ll**oon	_____	ba**ll**
p**u**rsue	_____	p**u**rse
she**r**i**ff**	_____	**r**i**ff**-**r**a**ff**
cat**e**gory	_____	s**e**ction

TEST YOURSELF

I. Check the correct pattern.

1. (a) alright,	(b) all right	(b)
2. (a) baloon,	(b) balloon	(b)
3. (a) pursuit,	(b) persuit	(a)
4. (a) sherrif,	(b) sheriff	(b)
5. (a) category,	(b) catagory	(a)
6. (a) tarrif,	(b) tariff	(b)

II. Recall the mnemonic for each word.

1. a**no**int _____ (a**n o**il)

2. r**idi**culous _____ (r**idi**cule)

3. bus**i**ness _____ (bu**sy**)

4. de**spa**ir _____ (de**spa**rate)

5. ba**ll**oon _____ (ba**ll**)

6. reco**mm**end _____ (co**mm**end)

7. rep**e**tition _____ (rep**e**at)

8. hol**i**day _____ (hol**y**)

9. sher**iff** _____ (r**iff-raff**)

10. a**ll** right _____ (a**ll** wrong)

11. emba**rr**a**ss**ed _____ (**two** robbers, Sing Sing, **ass**)

12. p**ur**suit _____ (p**ur**se)

13. vi**c**ious _____ (vi**c**e)

14. cat**e**gory _____ (s**e**ction)

15. ab**se**nce _____ (ab**se**nt)

16. de**s**cription _____ (de**s**cribe)

17. exhi**la**rate _____ (hi**la**rious)

18. indispens**able** _____ (**able** worker)

19. superintend**ent** _____ (**rent**)

20. se**i**ze _____   (ne**ck**)

21. para**ll**el _____   (**all** tracks)

22. insist**ent** _____   (**rent**)

23. depend**able** _____   (**able** worker)

24. fri**ca**ss**ee** _____   (**ca**sserole)

25. depend**ent** _____   (**rent**)

26. si**e**ge _____   (c**i**ty)

27. persist**ent** _____   (**rent**)

28. occu**rre**nce _____   (cu**rre**nt event)

29. ba**tt**a lion _____   (ba**tt**le)

30. in**o**culate _____   (inj**e**ct)

III. Decide on the missing crucial letters or letter, then rewrite the complete word.

1. i—o—ulate _____   (n,c)

2. a—right _____   (ll)

3. p—rsuit _____   (u)

4. occu—nce _____   (rre)

5. cat—gory _____   (e)

6. she—i— _____   (r,ff)

7. ba—oon _____   (ll)

8. indispens—ble _____   (a)

9. superintend—nt _____   (e)

10. depend—ble _____   (a)

11. persist—nt _____   (e)

12. ba—a—ion _____   (tt,l)

13. fri—a—ee _____   (c,ss)

14. re—o—end _____   (c,mm)

15. d—spair _____ (e)

16. insist—nt _____ (e)

17. para—e— _____ (ll,l)

18. a—oint _____ (n)

19. exhi—ration _____ (la)

20. bu—ness _____ (si)

21. depend—nt _____ (e)

22. s—ge _____ (ie)

23. vi—ious _____ (c)

24. abs—nce _____ (e)

25. r—diculous _____ (i)

26. s—ze _____ (ei)

27. ho—iday _____ (l)

28. d—scription _____ (e)

29. emba—a—ment _____ (rr,ss)

30. rep—tition _____ (e)

15

How to Manage Exceptions to the
Dropped -e Rules

PROBLEMS
develo**pm**ent *or* develo**pem**ent?
arg**um**ent *or* arg**uem**ent?
tr**ul**y *or* tr**uel**y?
ey**ei**ng *or* ey**i**ng?

SOLUTION
You know that final *e* is *dropped* before a suffix beginning with a vowel —

(as in *blame — blamable*)

You know, also, that final *e* is *retained* if the suffix begins with a consonant —

(as in *care — careful*)

And you know that certain *c* and *g* words are conspicuous exceptions to these rules —

(as in *peace — peaceable; manage — manageable;*
judge — judgment, etc.)

There are still other exceptions to, and side lights on, the dropped -e rules that it will pay us to consider.

1. How about *development*?
Words like *statement, refinement, encouragement,* etc., lead many literate people to spell it *developement* — and at first glance

102

this pattern looks far from impossible. However, realize that the original word is:

develop, *not* develope

There is no final e on the parent word, and so it is not a matter of keeping or dropping the e.

The only correct spelling, and the one you want to become visually accustomed to, is:

develo**pment** _____

2. Other *-pment* words

The same principle operates in two other words. Note, in each case, that the parent word does *not* end in e.

PARENT WORD	-*ment* WORD	
to envelop	envelo**pment**	_____
to equip	equi**pment**	_____

3. Six Exceptions

There are important exceptions to the principle that e is dropped before a vowel, retained before a consonant.
These are:

1. wise + -*dom* = wi**sd**om (no e) _____

2. due + -*ly* = d**ul**y (no e) _____

3. true + -*ly* = tr**ul**y (no e) _____

4. whole + -*ly* = who**lly** (no e) _____

5. argue + -*ment* = arg**um**ent (no e) _____

6. awe + -*ful* = a**wf**ul (no e) _____

(*Wholly,* if examined, looks peculiar, as does any word which does not seem to be pronounced the way it is spelled. But *wholly* is *whole* plus *-ly,* except that it is one of the six in which the e is dropped, resulting in *wholly.*)

4. What about *full-of-holes*?

Hole ends in e. Add y, a vowel, and the result, by the principle we are discussing, should be *holy.* But *holy* means *pious, virtuous, sacred*, etc. So if we mean *full-of-holes*, we keep the e, and write *holey*. Thus:

The *holy* man's clothing was *holey*.

5. And *sincerely*?

Though *sincerely* follows our principle perfectly, for some odd reason the misspelling *sincerly* is popular. Note that we start with *sincere* which ends in a final e. We then add a consonant suffix, *-ly*. Therefore we keep the e.

sincerely _____

6. *Eyeing* or *eying*?

This word is a law unto itself. Either spelling is correct — *eying* or *eyeing*, with neither having preference over the other. The past is of course *eyed*.

7. Then there are *mile* and *line* and *nine*

Mile and *line* are two more important exceptions. By the principle, the e should drop before *-age*, which begins with a vowel. But the e is kept.

mile + *-age* = mil**ea**ge (pronounced *MY-lij*) _____

line + *-age* = lin**ea**ge (pronounced *LIN-ee-ij*) _____

Lineage refers to someone's family tree — if the number of lines in print is meant, the spelling is *linage*, pronounced *LYNE-ij*.

As for *nine*, notice these forms:

nine + *-teen* = nin**et**een _____

nine + *-ty* = nin**et**y _____

nine + *-th* = ni**nth** _____

In *nineteen* and *ninety*, we follow the principle: keep the e before a consonant. In *ninth*, we have an exception — the e is dropped.

8. How about *acre*?

By our principle, *acre* + *-age* should produce *acrage*. Although the e of *acre* should be dropped before a vowel, it is, on the contrary, retained. Thus:

acre + *-age* = acr**ea**ge (pronounced *AY-ker-ij*) _____

9. Finally, consider *stage* and *cage*

Two more similar words could hardly be imagined — yet the first follows the dropped -e principle, the second is an exception, when the vowel *y* is added.

stage + -y = sta**gy** _____

cage + -y = cag**ey**   _____

Of course, in forms like *staged, caged, staging,* and *caging,* the e is regularly dropped.

Let us now review, and commit to visual memory, the important problem words of this chapter.

1. develo**pm**ent _____
2. envelo**pm**ent _____
3. equi**pm**ent _____
4. wi**sd**om _____
5. d**ul**y _____
6. tr**ul**y _____
7. who**ll**y _____
8. arg**um**ent _____
9. a**wf**ul _____
10. hol**ey** _____
    (full of holes)
11. sincer**el**y _____
12. e**yi**ng or
    e**yei**ng _____

13. mil**ea**ge _____
14. lin**ea**ge _____
    (*ancestry*)
15. lin**a**ge _____
    (*lines*)
16. nineteen _____
17. ninety _____
18. nin**th** _____
19. acr**ea**ge _____
20. sta**gy** _____
21. cag**ey** _____

TEST YOURSELF

Rewrite the following words with the indicated suffix.

1. develop + -*ment* _____   (develo**pm**ent)
2. envelop + -*ment* _____   (envelo**pm**ent)

3. equip + -*ment* _____ (equi**p**ment)

4. wise + -*dom* _____ (wi**sd**om)

5. due + -*ly* _____ (d**ul**y)

6. true + -*ly* _____ (tr**ul**y)

7. whole + -*ly* _____ (who**ll**y)

8. argue + -*ment* _____ (arg**um**ent)

9. awe + -*ful* _____ (a**wf**ul)

10. hole + -*y* _____ (hol**ey**)

11. sincere + -*ly* _____ (sincer**el**y)

12. eye + -*ing* _____ (e**yei**ng or e**yi**ng)

13. mile + -*age* _____ (mil**ea**ge)

14. line + -*age* _____ (lin**ea**ge)
    (ancestry)

15. line + -*age* _____ (li**n**age)
    (*lines*)

16. nine + -*teen* _____ (nin**et**een)

17. nine + -*ty* _____ (ninety)

18. nine + -*th* _____ (ni**nt**h)

19. acre + -*age* _____ (acr**ea**ge)

20. stage + -*y* _____ (sta**gy**)

21. cage + -*y* _____ (cag**ey**)

PRETEST
1. occa**ss**ional *or* occa**s**ional?
2. va**c**uum *or* va**cc**uum?
3. buy some station**a**ry *or* station**e**ry?
4. a man of princi**ples** *or* princi**pals**?
5. sep**e**rate *or* sep**a**rate?

MNEMONICS
1. (occa**ss**ional *or* occa**s**ional?)
Considering the pronunciation, there is no logical reason for misspelling this word — but misspelled it is, over and over, even by fairly sophisticated citizens of the country.

The popular, and *incorrect*, pattern contains a double *s*, thus: *occassional;* the purpose of an effective mnemonic will therefore be to highlight the need for one, and only one, *s* in the middle of the word.

This will not be difficult. Since spelling is tied up with pronunciation in OCCA<u>S</u>IONAL, let us do a little pronouncing.

Say these words aloud.

trea**s**ure   plea**s**ure

mea**s**ure   u**s**ual

You will note that the single *s* in these four words has the same sound exactly as the required single *s* in OCCA<u>S</u>IONAL — a kind of liquid or voiced *sh* sound. Such a liquid *sh* sound is generally spelled with only one *s*, not two. Once you understand this principle, all temptation to use a double *s* in OCCA<u>S</u>IONAL, OCCA<u>S</u>IONALLY, or OCCA<u>S</u>ION will vanish.

> *Correct spelling:* occa**s**ional _____

> *Mnemonic:*   pronunciation and spelling similar to
>   words like *pleasure, measure, treasure,*
>   *usual,* etc.

2. (vac**uum** *or* **va**cc**uum?)**

In this word, all logic tempts to a double c, and the probability is that you checked the second form. If so, you will be relieved to learn that you are in the numerous company of many other educated people who are similarly misled by logic; but as it happens, the correct pattern requires a single c — because VACUUM derives from the Latin verb *vacare,* to empty, from which same root also derive the English words *vacant, vacate, vacation, vacuous,* etc.

The obvious mnemonic, then, will be one that ties a confusing form to an easily spelled form of the same word — in this case, VACANT. VACANT means empty, and a VACUUM has been completely emptied of everything, including air.

> *Correct Spelling:* vacuum _____
>
> *Mnemonic:*   vacant

3. (buy some stationa**ry** *or* **station**e**ry?)**

Anything STATIONARY stands still — note the *a* in STATIONARY and in STAND.

On the other hand, STATIONERY means PAPER, envelopes, etc. Note the **ER** in STATIONERY and PAPER.

> *Correct Spelling*s stationary (stand) _____
>
> *and Mnemonics:*   stationery (paper) _____

4. (a man of principle**s** *or* **princi**pal**s?)**

A PRINCIPLE is a RULE — note the -le ending on both words.

PRINCIPAL, on the other hand, means MAIN — note the *a* in both words.

Thus: A principle in grammar (rule)
        Business principles (rules)
        The principal reason (main)
        Interest on his principal (main money)
        Principal of a school (main teacher)
        Principals in a play (main actors)
        Principals in a business transaction (main people)

Correct Spellings princi**ple** (rule) _____

and mnemonics: princip**al** (m**ai**n) _____

5. (sep**e**rate *or* sep**a**rate?)

Adults usually spell this word correctly — most grade and high school students misspell it. The important letter is the one following the *p*. This crucial letter is *a*, not *e*.

To highlight this crucial letter, remember that SE**PA**RATE means A**PA**RT — and associate the *pa* in both words.

Correct Spelling: se**pa**rate _____
(whether adjective or verb)

Mnemonic: a**pa**rt

MNEMONICS CHART

Correct Pattern		*Mnemonic*
1. occa**s**ional _____		trea**s**ure, etc.
2. va**c**uum _____		va**c**ant
3. station**ary** _____		st**a**nd
4. station**ery** _____		pap**er**
5. princi**ple** _____		ru**le**
6. princip**al** _____		m**a**in
7. se**pa**rate _____		a**pa**rt

TEST YOURSELF

I. Check the correct pattern.
1. (a) seperate, (b) separate   (b)
2. a man of (a) principle, (b) principal   (a)
3. something fixed is (a) stationery, (b) stationary   (b)
4. (a) vaccuum, (b) vacuum   (b)
5. (a) occasional, (b) occassional   (a)

II. Recall the mnemonic for each word.

1. station**ery** _____ (pap**er**)

2. station**ary** _____ (st**a**nd)

   3. principal _____   (main)

   4. principle _____   (rule)

   5. vacuum _____   (vacant)

   6. absence _____   (absent)

   7. repetition _____   (repeat)

   8. pursuit _____   (purse)

   9. separate _____   (apart)

  10. balloon _____   (ball)

  11. category _____   (section)

  12. all right _____   (all wrong)

  13. holiday _____   (holy)

  14. despair _____   (desperate)

  15. occasional _____   (measure)

  16. business _____   (busy)

  17. sheriff _____   (riff-raff)

  18. ridiculous _____   (ridicule)

  19. recommend _____   (commend)

  20. description _____   (describe)

III. Decide on the crucial missing letter or letters, then rewrite the complete word.

   1. va—uum _____   (c)

   2. station—ry (fixed) _____   (a)

   3. p—rsuit _____   (u)

   4. abs—nce _____   (e)

   5. ho—iday _____   (l)

   6. d—spair _____   (e)

   7. station—ry (paper) _____   (e)

8. occa—ional _____ (s)

9. sep—rate _____ (a)

10. sher— _____ (iff)

11. a—right _____ (ll; two words)

12. re—o—end _____ (c,mm)

13. princip— (chief) _____ (al)

14. princip— (general truth) _____ (le)

15. d—scription _____ (e)

16. r—diculous _____ (i)

17. bu—ness _____ (si)

18. cat—gory _____ (e)

19. ba—oon _____ (ll)

20. rep—tition _____ (e)

16

How to Decide Between *-ly* and *-ally*

PROBLEMS
artisti**cly** *or* artisti**cally**?
publi**cly** *or* publi**cally**?
inciden**tly** *or* inciden**tally**?
coo**ly** *or* coo**lly**?

SOLUTION
The ending *-ly* changes an adjective into an adverb.
For example:

ADJECTIVE	ADVERB	
sweet	sweetly	_____
close	closely	_____
clever	cleverly	_____
painful	painfully	_____
definite	definitely	_____
cool	coolly	_____
royal	royally	_____
beautiful	beautifully	_____

Now a close scrutiny of these forms will disclose important basic principles:

Point 21
The *-ly* ending is always added to the *adjective* form, never to any other form —

112

Point 22

If the adjective ends in *l*, *-ly* is tacked on to the complete adjective, producing an *-lly* form —

(as in *coolly, royally, beautifully, painfully, really,* etc.)

Let us see how these two points will solve most of our *-ly* problems.

Points 21 and 22 repeated

The ending *-ly* is always tacked on to the adjective form only. If the adjective form ends in *l*, the adverb will end in *-lly*.

Let me present a chart.

Charts are always forbidding, I know, and I have kept them at a minimum throughout this book.

But the following chart is the simplest, most effective way of driving home the basic principle that the *-ly* ending is added to the adjective only, never to the noun.

Examine the words and forms carefully, committing the adverbs to visual memory. And pay special attention to the sixth, seventh, eleventh, and fourteenth words — these starred adverbs are high on the list of commonly misspelled demons.

	NOUN	ADJECTIVE	ADVERB	
1.	grace	gracious	graciously	_____
2.	insanity	insane	insanely	_____
3.	happiness	happy	happily[1]	_____
4.	dizziness	dizzy	dizzily	_____
5.	evidence	evident	evidently	_____
* 6.	accident	accidental	*accident**ally**	_____
* 7.	incident	incidental	*incident**ally**	_____
8.	ornament	ornamental	ornamentally	_____
9.	confidence	confident	confidently	_____
10.	confidence	confidential	confidentially	_____

[1] *y* changes to *i* before adding *-ly.*

*11. reality   real   *really _____

12. beauty   beautiful   beautifully _____

13. experiment   experimental experimentally _____

*14. coolness   cool   *coolly _____

Are these principles 100 per cent operative? No exceptions?

It would be naïve, as you realize by now, to look for exception-free principles. But in this instance the exceptions are few and at a minimum.

Exception 1

If an adjective ends in *double l*, one *l* is dropped before the ending -*ly* is added, and thus a triple *l* (*lll*) is avoided.

For example:

dull — dully _____   ill — illy _____

full — fully _____

Only the *double-l adjectives* are the exceptions. Words like the following end in only one *l* and therefore follow Point 22:

skillful — skillfully _____   youthful — youthfully _____

truthful — truthfully _____   cool — coolly _____

etc.

Exception 2

The adjectives *whole, one, due,* and *true* drop the e before -*ly* is added (as we know from Chapter 15.)

whole — wholly _____   due — duly _____

one — only _____   true — truly _____

(Of course, there are also the -*ble* adjectives which drop e before adding -*ly*, such as *possible — possibly, incredible — incredibly, terrible — terribly*, but these offer no spelling problem to the literate person.)

What if an adjective ends in *-ic*?

Every once in a while, as we sift through the principles and inconsistencies of English spelling, we chance upon a trend that is simple, straightforward, and practically free of exceptions.

One such trend concerns adjectives ending in *-ic*, such as:

academic	automatic
anemic	emphatic
aristocratic	lyric
puristic	prophetic
acoustic	scholastic

A problem often arises when we wish to write these and similar words in the adverbial form.

academi**cly** *or* academi**cally**?
puristi**cly** *or* puristi**cally**?
automati**cly** *or* automati**cally**?
artisti**cly** *or* artisti**cally**?
publi**cly** *or* publi**cally**?

These are happy questions to answer.

They are happy questions, because we can find a short, to-the-point answer.

The answer is:

We always spell such words with the ending *-ally*.

Point 23

If an adjective ends in *-ic* always form the adverb by adding *-ally.* Thus:

academic**ally** _____	automatic**ally** _____
anemic**ally** _____	emphatic**ally** _____
aristocratic**ally** _____	lyric**ally** _____
puristic**ally** _____	prophetic**ally** _____
acoustic**ally** _____	scholastic**ally** _____
artistic**ally** _____	etc.

Always?
Well, almost always.
Publicly is the only important exception.

Get used to the appearance of *publicly*. _____

Then cast all doubts aside. Any other adverb based on an -*ic* adjective will end in -*ally*.

athletic**ally** _____   phlegmatic**ally** _____

romantic**ally** _____   systematic**ally** _____

So we revise *Point 23* to read:
If an adjective ends in -*ic*, form the adverb by adding -*ally*, except in the case of *public*, to which only -*ly* is added.
Therefore —
When you wish to add -*ly* —

1. Remember to attach it to the adjective form only:

    (accidental) accident**ally** _____

    (incidental) incident**ally** _____

2. If the adjective ends in *l*, add -*ly* directly:

(cool) coo**lly** _____   (royal) roya**lly** _____

(real) rea**lly** _____   (skillful) skillfu**lly** _____

3. Remember the exceptions:

du**lly** _____   on**ly** _____

fu**lly** _____   du**ly** _____

who**lly** _____   tru**ly** _____

4. If the adjective ends in -*ic*, add -*ally*:

rustic**ally** _____   puristic**ally** _____

artistic**ally** _____   romantic**ally** _____

5. Remember the exception:

        publi**cly** _____

With a full understanding of Points 21-23, plus a sharp visual memory of the words to which these points apply, you can no longer go wrong on any -*ly* word.

TEST YOURSELF

Write the adverbial (*-ly*) form for the following words.

1. artistic _____   (artistic**ally**)

2. public _____   (publi**cly**)

3. incident _____   (incident**ally**)

4. cool _____   (coo**lly**)

5. accident _____   (accident**ally**)

6. painful _____   (painfu**lly**)

7. dull _____   (du**lly**)

8. full _____   (fu**lly**)

9. royal _____   (roya**lly**)

10. real _____   (real**ly**)

11. happy _____   (happ**ily**)

12. evident _____   (evident**ly**)

13. confident _____   (confident**ly**)

14. confidential _____   (confidentia**lly**)

15. experimental _____   (experimenta**lly**)

16. monumental _____   (monumenta**lly**)

17. breezy _____   (breez**ily**)

18. skillful _____   (skillfu**lly**)

19. truthful _____   (truthfu**lly**)

20. whole _____   (who**lly**)

21. one _____   (o**nly**)

22. due _____   (d**uly**)

23. true _____   (tr**uly**)

24. academic _____   (academic**ally**)

25. rustic _____   (rusti**cally**)

26. aristocratic _____   (aristocrati**cally**)

27. acoustic _____   (acousti**cally**)

28. lyric _____   (lyri**cally**)

29. romantic _____   (romanti**cally**)

30. systematic _____   (systemati**cally**)

31. analytic _____   (analyti**cally**)

17

Second Review

We have dealt in Chapters 11–16, with six broad groups of spelling demons —

I. WORDS WHICH DROP A FINAL e WHEN A SUFFIX BEGINNING WITH A VOWEL IS ADDED.

come — coming _____ desire — desirable _____

love — lovable _____ stone — stony _____

like — likable _____ bone — bony _____

etc.

II. WORDS WHICH RETAIN A FINAL e AFTER THE LETTER c WHEN THE SUFFIX -able IS ADDED.

noticeable _____ peaceable _____

serviceable _____ pronounceable _____

irreplaceable _____ traceable _____

etc.

III. WORDS WHICH INSERT A -k AFTER FINAL c WHEN A SUFFIX BEGINNING WITH e, i, OR y IS ADDED.

panic — panicky _____ mimic — mimicked _____

traffic — trafficker _____ picnic — picnicking _____

frolic — frolicking _____ physic — physicked _____

etc.

IV. WORDS WHICH RETAIN A FINAL *e* AFTER THE LETTER *g* WHEN THE SUFFIX *-able* OR *-ous* IS ADDED.

changeable _____   marriageable _____

manageable _____   salvageable _____

outrageous _____   courageous _____

etc.

V. WORDS WHICH PREFERABLY DROP FINAL *e* AFTER *dg* WHEN *-ment* IS ADDED.

judgment _____   abridgment _____

lodgment _____   acknowledgment _____

etc.

VI. ADJECTIVES WHICH END IN *-ic* AND ADD *-ally* FOR ADVERBIAL FORMS.

rustic — rustically _____   analytic — analytically _____

artistic — artistically _____   lyric — lyrically _____

etc.

In addition, we have discussed a number of other basic principles:

1. Final *-e* is retained when a suffix beginning with a consonant is added:

care — careful _____   like — likeness _____

vague — vaguely _____   refine — refinement _____

etc.

2. If a word ends in *-dge*, final *-e* is retained before adding *-able*, even though a preceding *d* normally keeps a *g* soft:

knowledgeable _____   abridgeable _____

etc.

3. No *-e* is added before *-ment* if the original word ended in a consonant:

develop — development _____   equip — equipment _____

envelop — envelo**pm**ent _____ embarrass —

embarra**ss**ment _____

etc.

4. Certain exceptional words drop final -e when a consonant beginning with a suffix is added:

wise — wi**sd**om _____ whole — who**ll**y _____

due — d**ul**y _____ argue — arg**um**ent _____

true — tr**ul**y _____ awe — a**wf**ul _____

5. The word *hole* retains final -e before -y is added to distinguish it from *holy*:

(full of holes) hol**ey** _____ (pious) hol**y** _____

6. *Mile, line,* and *acre* retain final -e before adding -*age*:

mil**e**age _____ lin**e**age _____

acr**e**age _____   (if it means *family descent,* otherwise *linage*)

7. *Nine* drops final -e before -*th*, retains it before -*teen* and -*ty*.

ni**nt**h _____ nin**e**teen _____

nin**e**ty _____

8. *Stage* drops final -e before adding -y; *cage* retains it.

stage — sta**gy** _____ cage — cag**ey** _____

9. *Eye* may optionally either drop or retain final -e before -*ing:*

ey**i**ng _____ or eye**i**ng _____

10. If an adjective ends in *l*, the adverb will end in -*lly:*

accident**al** — incident**al** —

   accident**ally** _____   incident**ally** _____

cool — coo**ll**y _____ real — rea**ll**y _____

etc.

11. If an adjective ends in *ll*, the adverbs end in -*lly:*

fu**ll** — fu**lly** _____ du**ll** — du**lly** _____

etc.

12. *Public* alone, among the hundreds of common *-ic* adjectives, adds only *-ly* to form an adverb:

public — publi**cly** _____

13. When *-or* is added to mortgage, final *-e* is dropped:

mortga**gor** _____

SECOND REVIEW TEST

I. Add the indicated suffix to each word, rewriting in the blank space.

1. like + -*able* _____ (likable)

2. value + -*able* _____ (valuable)

3. desire + -*able* _____ (desirable)

4. love + -*able* _____ (lovable)

5. give + -*ing* _____ (giving)

6. size + -*able* _____ (sizable)

7. argue + -*ing* _____ (arguing)

8. care + -*ful* _____ (careful)

9. notice + -*able* _____ (noticeable)

10. service + -*able* _____ (serviceable)

11. enforce + -*able* _____ (enforceable)

12. enforce + -*ment* _____ (enforcement)

13. embrace + -*ing* _____ (embracing)

14. use + -*able* _____ (usable)

15. panic + -*y* _____ (panicky)

16. mimic + -*ry* _____ (mimicry)

17. mimic + -*ing* _____ (mimicking)

18. frolic + -*ed* _____ (frolicked)

19. colic + -*y* _____ (colicky)

20. change + -*able* _____ (changeable)

21. knowledge + -*able* _____ (knowledgeable)

22. mortgage + -*or* _____ (mortgagor)

23. judge + -*ment* _____ (judgment)

24. acknowledge + -*ment* _____ (acknowledgment)

25. engage + -*ment* _____ (engagement)

26. outrage + -*ous* _____ (outrageous)

27. courage + -*ous* _____ (courageous)

28. develop + -*ment* _____ (development)

29. equip + -*ment* _____ (equipment)

30. wise + -*dom* _____ (wisdom)

31. due + -*ly* _____ (duly)

32. true + -*ly* _____ (truly)

33. whole + -*ly* _____ (wholly)

34. argue + -*ment* _____ (argument)

35. awe + -*ful* _____ (awful)

36. hole + -*y* _____ (holey)

37. sincere + -*ly* _____ (sincerely)

38. mile + -*age* _____ (mileage)

39. line + -*age* _____ (lineage)
    (ancestry)

40. line + -*age* _____ (linage)
    (lines in print)

41. nine + -*th* _____ (ninth)

42. nine + -*ty* _____ (ninety)

43. nine + -*teen* _____ (nineteen)

44. acre + -*age* _____ (acreage)

45. stage + -*y* _____ (stagy)

46. cage + -y _____ (cagey)

47. accident + -*ly* _____ (accidentally)

48. incident + -*ly* _____ (incidentally)

49. evident + -*ly* _____ (evidently)

50. painful + -*ly* _____ (painfully)

51. royal + -*ly* _____ (royally)

52. cool + -*ly* _____ (coolly)

53. full + -*ly* _____ (fully)

54. experiment + -*ly* _____ (experimentally)

55. artistic + -*ly* _____ (artistically)

56. public + -*ly* _____ (publicly)

57. scholastic + -*ly* _____ (scholastically)

58. puristic + -*ly* _____ (puristically)

18

(Twelfth Day)

How to Decide Between *c* and *s* in the Ending of a Word

PROBLEMS

  prophe**c**y *or* prophe**s**y?
  ecsta**c**y *or* ecsta**s**y?
  preten**c**e *or* preten**s**e?
  licen**c**e *or* licen**s**e?

SOLUTION

No literate Spaniard ever has trouble with the spelling of Spanish words.

Ditto for the literate Italian.

For in these two languages, among others, a word is generally spelled the way it sounds, and sounds the way it is spelled.

Not so, as you have long since discovered, in English.

The letter *s*, for example, may have any number of sounds.

It may sound like *sh*, as in *sure* and *sugar*.

It may sound like *z*, as in *miser*.

It may sound like *zh*, as in *leisure* or *measure*.

It can be silent, as in *viscount*.

Or take *c*. It can be hard, as in *cat;* soft, as in *city;* like a *ch*, as in *cello;* like *sh*, as in *appreciate;* or even silent, as in *indict*.

That's just a small indication of what you're up against when you attempt to spell English words.

And it works the other way around.

125

A single sound can have two or more different spellings. The sound "seed," as you know, may be spelled -*sede* as in *supersede;* -*cede* as in *accede;* -*ceed* as in *proceed. Sea* and *see* are identical in sound, and so are *there* and *their* and *they're; to, too, two; been* and *bin; stationary* and *stationery; die* and *dye;* and so on and on and on.

A similar occurrence (and therein lies the problem) is found in words which end with the syllable that sounds like "see."

For example, *vacancy.*

Vacancy ends in -*cy.*

For further example, *ecstasy.*

Ecstasy, with the same final sound, ends in -*sy.*

How can we ever know which is which?

The problem begins to sound complicated.

But even a complicated problem can be made simple and can be quickly and effectively solved if we attack it dynamically.

The -*cy-or-sy* problem is no exception.

First let us discover exactly where the problem occurs.

No normal speller is ever tempted to write -sy where -cy is required. There are words, however, in which he is tempted to make the opposite substitution — using -*cy* in place of the correct -*sy.*

How many such words?

Generally no more than four.

These four, acceptable only with an -*sy* ending, are:

ecstasy _____   hypocrisy _____

idiosyncrasy _____   apostasy _____

(An *apostate* has forsaken his religion, faith, principles, or political affiliations. He is a kind of turncoat, a traitor to his previous cause or beliefs. *Apostasy,* then, is the noun that describes the apostate's desertion.)

Ecstasy, idiosyncrasy, hypocrisy, and *apostasy* are of course not by any means the only English words ending in -*sy* — *but they are the only ones likely to cause confusion or to be unconsciously misspelled.* Words like *pleurisy, heresy, argosy, courtesy, fantasy* also end in -*sy* — but there is no tendency even among comparatively poor spellers to end them with -*cy.*

So an apparently complicated problem is in actuality relatively simple.

Become visually and kinesthetically adjusted to the pattern of four words:

ecsta**s**y _____ hypocri**s**y _____

idiosyncra**s**y _____ aposta**s**y _____

And then set your doubts at rest. In all other words you will naturally use the correct ending.

Speaking of -sy and -cy, this is as good a time as any to consider the confusing words *prophesy* and *prophecy*.

> *prophesy* is pronounced *PROFF-e-sigh*
> *prophecy* is pronounced *PROFF-e-see*

Prophesy (*PROFF-e-sigh*) is a verb, and has the usual verb forms:

To *prophesy* a real-estate boom.
He *prophesied* a real-estate boom. (*PROFF-e-sighed*)
She *prophesies* a real-estate boom. (*PROFF-e-sighs*)
We are *prophesying* a real-estate boom. (*PROFF-e-sigh-ing*)

Prophecy (*PROFF-e-see*) is a noun, with the usual plural form:
One *prophecy* (*PROFF-e-see*)
Many *prophecies* (*PROFF-e-sees*)
What about *prophecize?*
There is simply no such word — although it may occasionally be heard as an erroneous substitute for the verb to *prophesy*.

As in the case of -cy and -sy, the problem of whether to end a word with -ence or -ense is deceptively complicated, but actually very simple.

Most words in which there is any possibility of a choice end in -ence: *benevolence, consequence, difference, experience*, etc., etc. And rarely does anyone write -ense where -ence is required.

But in four special instances, there is a strong temptation to substitute -ence for the preferable -ense.

These four instances are:

pret**ense** _____ def**ense** _____

off**ense** _____ lic**ense** _____

(British usage, strangely enough, accepts the -*ence* ending in these words — but the only absolutely safe American spelling of these forms is -*ense*.)

You will have no difficulty separating *pretense, offense, defense,* and *license* from the vast number of -*ence* words if you consider their easily spelled longer forms. Namely:

pretense — pretension   defense — defensive
offense — offensive   license — licensing

Here again, you need only become visually and kinesthetically adjusted to four special words, and the problem is automatically solved. In all others you will naturally and without hesitation make the correct choice between -*ence* and -*ense*.

For most words in which a choice is possible end in -*ence* —

And the few other words (besides the special four I have mentioned) which end in -*ense* (such as *expense, intense, dispense, suspense,* etc.) cause no trouble.

Let me offer the special cases once more for further visual and kinesthetic practice.

pret**ense** _____   def**ense** _____

off**ense** _____   lic**ense** _____

We can now sum up the solutions to the chapter problems by formulating four basic principles:

Point 24

In choosing between -*cy* and -*sy*, bear in mind four special words: *ecstasy, hypocrisy, idiosyncrasy,* and *apostasy.*

Point 25

Differentiate between *prophesy* and *prophecy* by using the -*sy* form as a verb, the -*cy* form as a noun. Remember that *prophesy* is pronounced *PROFF-e-sigh, prophecy* is pronounced *PROFF-e-see.*

Point 26

In choosing between -*ence* and -*ense*, again bear in mind four special words: *pretense, offense, defense,* and *license.*

Point 27

With this background, you should normally not encounter any problems. Other -*cy-sy* and -*ence-ense* forms rarely if ever cause trouble.

TEST YOURSELF

I. Add -cy or -sy, as required, to the following forms, rewriting the complete word.

1. ecsta — _____ (sy)

2. idiosyncra — _____ (sy)

3. aposta — _____ (sy)

4. hypocri — _____ (sy)

5. vacan — _____ (cy)

6. courte — _____ (sy)

7. to prophe — _____ (sy)
   (verb)

8. a foolish prophe — _____ (cy)
   (noun)

9. priva — _____ (cy)

10. diploma — _____ (cy)

II. Add -ce or -se to the following forms, rewriting the complete word.

1. defen — _____ (se)

2. offen — _____ (se)

3. licen — _____ (se)

4. preten — _____ (se)

5. suspen — _____ (se)

6. expen — _____ (se)

7. experien — _____ (ce)

8. impertinen — _____ (ce)

9. dispen — _____ (se)

10. inten — _____ (se)

19

How to Decide Between
-*ify* and -*efy*

PROBLEMS
> liqu**i**fy *or* liqu**e**fy?
> rar**i**fy *or* rar**e**fy?
> stup**i**fy *or* stup**e**fy?
> putr**i**fy *or* putr**e**fy?

SOLUTION

The four problem words of this chapter are among the forms generally misspelled by even the most literate and educated of writers.

What makes these words so troublesome? Why do so many educated people misspell them without any realization of error? (You will find many stubborn souls so certain that the *incorrect* form is correct that they will bet money on it!)

The answer is simple.

If there is a choice, practically every similar word ends in -*ify*, not -*efy*.

For instance:

classify	edify
codify	qualify
crucify	testify

And so on, scores and scores of them.

Every word, that is, *except the four problem words that start this chapter.*

Point 28

These four, and only these four among problem words, end in
-efy[1].

1. liquefy _____   3. stupefy _____

2. rarefy _____   4. putrefy _____

And of course other forms of these words follow the same pattern.

liquefying _____   rarefied _____

liquefied _____   rarefies _____

liquefies _____   stupefying _____

liquefaction _____   stupefied _____

rarefying _____   stupefies _____

stupefaction _____   putrefies _____

putrefying _____   putrefaction _____

putrefied _____   etc.

How can you remember that these four alone end in -efy?

There will be no difficulty. A few moments devoted to committing
them to visual memory and to kinesthetic practice will solve your
problem.

For exceptions, as you have probably learned, are easy to
remember.

(Remember *supersede, procedure, paralyze, analyze, leisure,
weird, seize. mortgagor,* etc.?)

Keep *liquefy, rarefy, stupefy,* and *putrefy* in mind, not so that
you can repeat them in order, necessarily, but only so that you
will recall them as exceptions when you have to write them —

And then spell, as you naturally would anyway, any other word
with the natural ending -ify.

[1]There are also, for example, *defy,* which offers no spelling problem,
and *torrefy,* a rather obscure word meaning *to subject to heat. Torrify,*
however, is also acceptable.

MNEMONICS
Seven

PRETEST
1. acce**ll**erate *or* accelerate?
2. d**e**vise *or* d**i**vise?
3. i**rr**idescent *or* iridescent?
4. tranqui**l**ity *or* tranqui**ll**ity?
5. gramm**er** *or* gramm**ar**?

MNEMONICS

1. (acce**ll**erate *or* accelerate?)

There is some temptation here to double the *l*, as the second syllable receives the accent. The correct spelling is best remembered by analogy with another form, CELERITY. ACCELERATE means *to speed up*, CELERITY means *speed* — both are derived from the same Latin root, *celer*, fast.

> *Correct Spelling:* accelerate _____
>
> *Mnemonic:*   celerity

2. (d**e**vise *or* d**i**vise?)

This demon sounds like *divise*, and by analogy with *divide* seems an eminently sensible pattern. However, only DEVISE is correct; to remember the crucial *e*, use a mnemonic that ties a difficult form of a word to an easily spelled form, as we did in DESCRIPTION — DESCRIBE. The adjective form of DEVISE is DEVIOUS, impossible to misspell since the pronunciation (*DEE-ve-us*) demands an *e* for the first vowel.

> *Correct Spelling:* d**e**vise _____
>
> *Mnemonic:*   devious

(The noun form, DEVICE, has the same second letter as DEVISE.)

3. (irridescent *or* iridescent?)

This word means *having a rainbow of colors*, and derives from the Greek root *iris*, rainbow. There is also an *iris* in the eye, derived from the same root; and because of the pronunciation of *iris* (*EYE-ris*), there is no temptation to double the r. In IRIDES-CENT (pronounced *ir-i-DESS-ent*), the pronunciation does tempt to a double r, but the mnemonic IRIS will help you avoid that common pitfall.

> *Correct Spelling:* iridescent _____
>
> *Mnemonic:*   iris

4. (tranquility *or* tranquillity?)

The preferable spelling contains a double *l* — think that in the old days life had (so they say) far more TRAN**QUILL**ITY than today; and those were the days, also, when people wrote with *QUILLS* rather than ball-point pens.

> *Preferable Spelling:* tran**quill**ity _____
>
> *Mnemonic:*   **quill**

(The base word, of course, is spelled TRANQUI**L**.)

5. (grammer *or* grammar?)

The pronunciation is indeed *GRAM-mer*, and so tempts to misspelling. Keep in mind that poor GRAM**MAR MARS** your speech.

> *Correct Spelling:* gram**mar** _____
>
> *Mnemonic:*   **mar**

MNEMONICS CHART

Correct Pattern	*Mnemonic*
1. accelerate _____	celerity
2. devise _____	devious
3. iridescent _____	iris
4. tranquillity _____	quill
5. grammar _____	mar

TEST YOURSELF

I. Check the correct or preferable pattern.

1. (a) grammer,   (b) grammar.   (b)
2. (a) accellerate, (b) accelerate   (b)
3. (a) tranquillity, (b) tranquility   (a)
4. (a) divise,   (b) devise.   (b)
5. (a) irridescent, (b) iridescent   (b)

II. Recall the mnemonic for each word.

1. gram**mar** _____ (**mar**)

2. **ir**idescent _____ (**iris**)

3. acce**ler**ate _____ (celerity)

4. **devi**se _____ (devious)

5. tran**quill**ity _____ (**quill**)

6. ba**ll**oon _____ (ba**ll**)

7. cate**g**ory _____ (section)

8. station**er**y _____ (pap**er**)

9. ab**se**nce _____ (ab**se**nt)

10. p**ur**suit _____ (p**ur**se)

11. occa**s**ional _____ (mea**s**ure)

12. va**c**uum _____ (va**c**ant)

13. she**riff** _____ (**riff-raff**)

14. ho**li**day _____ (ho**l**y)

15. station**a**ry _____ (st**a**nd)

16. princip**al** _____ (m**a**in)

17. **all** right _____ (**all** wrong)

18. princi**ple** _____ (ru**le**)

19. sep**a**rate _____ (**apa**rt)

20. de**s**pair _____ (de**s**perate)

III. Decide on the crucial missing letters, then rewrite the complete word.

1. d— vise _____ (e)

2. station — ry (supplies) _____ (e)

3. p— rsuit _____ (u)

4. va — uum _____ (c)

5. sher — _____ (iff)

6. occa — ional _____ (s)

7. ho — iday _____ (l)

8. gramm — r _____ (a)

9. abs — nce _____ (e)

10. ba — oon _____ (ll)

11. princip — (chief) _____ (al)

12. a — right _____ (ll)

13. i— idescent _____ (r)

14. d — spair _____ (e)

15. princip — (truth) _____ (le)

16. acce — erate _____ (l)

17. cat — gory _____ (e)

18. station — ry (fixed) _____ (a)

19. sep — rate _____ (a)

20. tranqui — ity _____ (ll)

20

When to Double a Consonant and When to Leave It Alone

PROBLEM

gases *or* gasses?
buses *or* busses?
quizes *or* quizzes?

SOLUTION

Of course you can spell *gas.*

You can spell *bus.*

You can spell *quiz, regret, refer, travel, begin, equip.*

There is usually no problem in these words — they are spelled pretty much the way they are pronounced, a refreshing and (you may feel) a relatively rare circumstance.

The problem arises when you want to use a longer form of any of these or similar words: *gases* or *gasses? buses* or *busses? quizes* or *quizzes? regretable* or *regrettable? refering* or *referring? traveler* or *traveller? begining* or *beginning? equiped* or *equipped?*

And it is a problem that arises again and again.

In fact, it is one of the commonest and most plaguing of spelling problems — *when to double a consonant and when to leave it alone.*

You know what a consonant is? A consonant is any of twenty letters of the alphabet: *b, c, d, f, g, h, j, k, l, m, n, p, q, r, s, t, v, w, x, z.*

In other words, it is any letter other than one of the six vowels: *a, e, i, o, u, y.* (You will recall that we consider *y* the sixth vowel.)

There is a comparatively reliable but painfully complicated principle that covers the problem.

138

It is, I repeat, a painfully complicated principle — and if I were so reckless as to present it baldly and without considerable preparation you might run the risk of becoming hopelessly confused and discouraged.

So valuable is the principle, however; so easy to apply when it is clearly and thoroughly understood; and so far-reaching in its influence over many hundreds of words which perplex the average speller, that we want to explore it deeply and completely.

So we shall take the principle apart, study it piece by piece, understand every ramification of it, apply it in scores of practical situations, and thereby become so familiar with it that its complexity will vanish and all possibility of attendant pain will be avoided.

First

Our doubling principle applies largely to *verbs*.

A *verb*, as you may know, is a word that shows action, like

to grab	to stop
to swim	to bag
to run	to hop
to blur	to twit
to quiz	to trot

The ten verbs I have offered as examples contain, it so happens, only one syllable. But the principle applies just as effectively to verbs of any number of syllables, though most of the examples will be of one to three syllables in length. For example:

to control	to travel
to repel	to develop
to regret	to inhibit
to refer	to disinter
to benefit	

Second

Our interest in this chapter will for a time center on *one-syllable verbs* of a very special type. You have already been exposed to ten examples of this type of verb (*grab, swim, run, trot,* etc.) and possibly you have noticed a common and most important element.

Each such verb ended in a single consonant.

Here are some similar verbs; the single, final consonant is printed in heavy type.

to quit	to skip
to plan	to drum
to char	to wet

Now examine once again the sixteen one-syllable verbs I have offered.

You will notice a second common and important element — *each final single consonant is preceded by a single vowel.* This single vowel is printed in heavy type.

grab	twit
swim	trot
run	quit[1]
blur	plan
quiz[1]	char
stop	skip
bag	drum
hop	wet

All right — we've got two important points to consider. If a one-syllable verb

1. *ends in a single consonant*
2. *preceded by a single vowel*

Then —
You double the final consonant before adding a suffix.
Any kind of suffix?
No — but don't worry about that for just a moment.
Now watch how we double the final consonant before adding a suffix.

grab + -*ing* = grabbing _____

swim + -*er* = swimmer _____

run + -*ing* = running _____

blur + -*ed* = blurred _____

[1] In the case of *quiz* and *quit*, the *u* is pronounced like W (*KWIZ, KWIT*) and so does not function as a vowel.

quiz + -es = quizzes[2] _____

quiz + -ed = quizzed[2] _____

quiz + -ing = quizzing[2] _____

stop + -ing = stopping _____

hop + -ing = hopping _____

twit + -ing = twitting _____

trot + -er = trotter _____

quit + -er = quitter _____

plan + -ed = planned _____

char + -ed = charred _____

skip + -ed = skipped _____

drum + -er = drummer _____

wet + -ing = wetting _____

I have asked whether this principle operates when any kind of suffix is added — and I have answered no, not any kind.

The suffixes we have added in the preceding list were -ing, -ed, -es, or -er.

In short, suffixes starting with a vowel.

Now this is all simple enough, and probably the only words you might have misspelled, if any, were *quizzes, quizzed* and *quizzing* — but don't become impatient. This material, so far, is all introductory, intended as essential preparation for harder and more important applications of the doubling principle.

If we go very slow, bit by bit, if we take it easy, adequately preparing every step of the way, you will shortly, and painlessly, become an expert on the complete and complicated doubling principle.

So let us now state what we know so far.

[2] Of all these and similar words, *quizzes, quizzed* and *quizzing* are the most likely to be misspelled, often appearing, incorrectly, with a single z.

Point 29

If a one-syllable word (usually a verb) —

Ends in a *single* consonant —

(like gra**b**)

Preceded by a *single* vowel —

(gr**a**b)

You double the final consonant —

Before adding a suffix —

Which begins with a vowel.

(grab + -*ing* = grabbing).

(You see how involved it already sounds — but you understand it so far because of the careful, step-by-step preparation. And this is only *part* of the doubling principle!)

If a suffix begins with a consonant, such as -*ness*, -*ly*, -*ful*, or -*ment*, the principle does not hold.

$$wet + -ness = wetness$$
$$thin + -ness = thinness$$

(We have not doubled the final *n*, but only combined the *n* of *thin* with the *n* of -*ness*.)

$$man + -ly = manly$$
$$drum + -ful = drumful$$
$$ship + -ment = shipment$$

Now consider, as special cases (in English spelling there are almost always special cases) —

gas and *bus*

Both *gas* and *bus* end in single consonants preceded by single vowels.

In the case of *gas*, when we add -*ed* or -*ing*, we follow the doubling principle exactly as described — we double the *s*.

gassed _____

gassing _____

But —

(And now you will further understand why English spelling is such a headache, why it causes so much insecurity.)

With other suffixes, such as *-es, -eous, -ify, we do not double*
the s — even though these suffixes also, like *-ed* and *-ing*, start
with a vowel.

gases _____

gaseous _____
(pronounced *GAS-ee-us*)

gasify _____

gasifiable _____

gasifier _____

gasification _____

Only *gassed* and *gassing* follow the doubling principle — other
forms are exceptions.

In the case of *bus*, you may double the *s* or not, as you choose,
before adding *-es*.

Either buses _____

or busses _____

(Neither is the preferable form, though *buses* is seen more frequently and is the only spelling used by the *New York Times*. *Bus*
is a shortened form of *omnibus*, and so it is not originally a one-
syllable word — and the location of the accent in *omnibus* is, as
you will learn in a later chapter, the factor which influences the
single *s.*)

However, *bussed* and *bussing* (that is, using a *bus*, not forms of
buss, to kiss) are the usual spellings.

So we might conclude with a final point.

Point 30

In *gases, gaseous, gasify*, etc., the final *s* of *gas* is not doubled,
though in *gassed* and *gassing* it is.   Either *buses* or *busses* is
acceptable.

This chapter has given you the essential preparation you need
for harder and more important work ahead — work that deals with
the complex concept of *accent*.   Before getting into any more
trouble, however, test your understanding of what we have already
discussed.

TEST YOURSELF

I. Add the indicated suffix to the following words, then rewrite.

1. blur + -*ed* _____ (blu**rr**ed)

2. rob + -*ed* _____ (ro**bb**ed)

3. can + -*ing* _____ (ca**nn**ing)

4. run + -*er* _____ (ru**nn**er)

5. sob + -*ing* _____ (so**bb**ing)

6. thin + -*er* _____ (thi**nn**er)

7. thin + -*ness* _____ (thi**nn**ess)

8. quiz + -*es* _____ (qui**zz**es)

9. quiz + -*ed* _____ (qui**zz**ed)

10. quiz + -*ing* _____ (qui**zz**ing)

11. quiz + -*ical* _____ (qui**zz**ical)

12. gas + -*es* _____ (ga**s**es)

13. gas + -*ed* _____ (ga**ss**ed)

14. gas + -*ing* _____ (ga**ss**ing)

15. gas + -*eous* _____ (ga**s**eous)

16. gas + -*ify* _____ (ga**s**ify)

17. ship + -*ing* _____ (shi**pp**ing)

18. ship + -*ment* _____ (shipment)

19. twit + -*ed* _____ (twi**tt**ed)

20. scar + -*ed* _____ (sca**rr**ed)

21. lap + -*ing* _____ (la**pp**ing)

22. skin + -*er* _____ (ski**nn**er)

23. drum + -*ed* _____ (dru**mm**ed)

24. drum + -*ful* _____ (dru**m**ful)

25. bus + -*es* _____ (bu**s**es or
bu**ss**es)

When to Double a *t*

PROBLEM
 alloted *or* allotted?
 benefited *or* benefitted?

SOLUTION
 We have learned, then, under Point 29, that:
 In a one-syllable word which ends in a single consonant—
 Preceded by a *single vowel*—
 The final consonant is doubled before adding a suffix—
 If that suffix starts with a *vowel*.
As applied to one-syllable words, that is as much of the doubling principle as you have to know.

But since most spelling problems occur when suffixes are added to two- and three-syllable words (usually verbs), there are further ramifications and qualifications of the doubling principle with which you will wish to become thoroughly and comfortably familiar.

Purely for the sake of simplicity, let us concentrate, in this chapter, on words of two or three syllables which end in the letter *t*—but bear in mind that anything you learn will apply with equal force to all similar words no matter what the final consonant.

Our doubling principle still applies only to *words which end in a single consonant preceded by a single vowel.* Consider these special examples:

GROUP I

to acquit	to allot
to commit	to regret
to abet	to abut
to forget	to admit
to beset	to transmit

In addition to the common ending (the final single consonant, preceded by a single vowel), these words have another common characteristic.

All of them are accented on the last syllable.

We say:

ac-*QUIT*	al-*LOT*
com-*MIT*	re-*GRET*
a-*BET*	a-*BUT*
for-*GET*	ad-*MIT*
bc-*SET*	trans-*MIT*

Such words are different, in this important particular, from the following examples, which are *not accented on the last syllable.*

GROUP II

to banquet — *BANG-quet*
to covet — *KUV-et*
to benefit — *BEN-e-fit*
to merit — *MER-it*
to profit — *PROF-it*
to prohibit — *pro-HIB-it*
to inhibit — *in-HIB-it*
to discomfit — *diss-KUM-fit*
to rivet — *RIV-et*
to visit — *VIZ-it*

This point of difference is most crucial. Though both sets of words end in a single consonant preceded by a single vowel —

One set is accented on the final syllable (Group I).

The other set is accented *on some syllable other than the final one* (Group II).

And the doubling principle applies, in the case of two- or three-syllable words, *only to those accented on the final syllable.*

That is, only to words of the type illustrated in Group I.

So —

Let us now add suffixes to the words in Group I, remembering —

That we double the final consonant if —

1. The word ends in *a single consonant*
2. Preceded by *a single vowel*

3. And is accented *on the final syllable*

4. And, moreover, the suffix to be added starts with *a vowel.*

These are, as you will recall, the same conditions required, as we discussed them in Chapter 20, for doubling in one-syllable words — *with the important addition of final syllable accent.*

DOUBLE THE FINAL CONSONANT

acquit' + -ing = acquitting _____

commit' + -ed = committed _____

abet' + -ing = abetting _____

(un)forget' + -able = unforgettable _____

beset' + -ing = besetting _____

allot' + -ed = allotted _____

regret' + -able = regrettable _____

abut' + -ed = abutted _____

admit' + -ance = admittance _____

transmit' + -al = transmittal _____

If we add a suffix beginning with a *consonant*, we do not, of course, double.

DO NOT DOUBLE THE FINAL CONSONANT

commit' + -ment = commitment _____

allot' + -ment = allotment _____

regret' + -ful = regretful _____

abut' + -ment = abutment _____

And if the word is of the type in Group II, with the accent *on other than the final syllable*, we again do not double.

DO NOT DOUBLE THE FINAL CONSONANT

ban'quet + -ing = banqueting _____

cov'et + -ous = covetous _____

ben' efit + -ed = benefited _____

mer' it + -ing = meriting _____

prof' it + -ing = profiting _____

prohib' it + -ed = prohibited _____

inhib' it + -ing = inhibiting _____

discom' fit + -ing = discomfiting _____

riv' et + -er = riveter _____

vis' it + -ed = visited _____

Well, how does it look so far?

The doubling principle is gradually becoming more and more elaborate — but with the preparation you have had it should no longer sound too complicated.

We still do not have the entire formula for doubling final consonants — but let us gather what items we are now familiar with into a basic principle:

Point 31

If a word of more than one syllable —
Ends in *a single consonant* —
  (permit)
Preceded by *a single vowel* —
  (permit)
And receives the accent *on the last syllable* —
  (per-mit')
Double the final consonant —
When adding a suffix that starts with *a vowel.*
  (per-mit' + -ed = permitted)

No special cases?

But of course — there almost always are special cases.

Take *ricochet* and *crochet.*

Ricochet and *crochet* satisfy all the requirements of the doubling principle.

They both end in single consonants preceded by single vowels —
And the accent is on the last syllable.

But their pronunciation is unusual — the final *t* is silent:

> ricochet — *rick-o-SHAY*
> crochet — *cro-SHAY*

Both words are directly derived from French, in which interesting language -*et* is pronounced *ay*.

And in both words, or any similar ones in which final -*et* is pronounced *ay*, *we do not double the t before a suffix*.

ricochet + -ing = ricocheting _____

ricochet + -ed = ricocheted _____

crochet + -ing = crocheting _____

crochet + -ed = crocheted _____

crochet + -er = crocheter _____

These words are pronounced:

> ricocheting — *rick-o-SHAY-ing*
> ricocheted — *rick-o-SHAYD*
> crocheting — *cro-SHAY-ing*
> crocheted — *cro-SHAYD*
> crocheter — *cro-SHAY-er*

We can thus add a new principle:

Point 32

If final *t* is silent, as in *ricochet* and *crochet*, do not double the final consonant when adding a suffix.

Or take, as another very special case, to *outfit*.

Outfit, as a verb, is pronounced *OUT'-fit*, with the accent on the first syllable.

It thus violates one of the requirements of the doubling principle, even though it satisfies all the others.

Nevertheless, the *t* is doubled before a suffix beginning with a vowel.

outfitting _____

outfitted _____

outfitter _____

The reason is fairly obvious.

Actually, this is the verb *fit* plus a special prefix.

So we operate under the principle that applies to one-syllable words, disregarding the position of the accent.

Similar words offer no problem, since the accent falls on the last syllable.

For example:

> *out-RUN'* — outru**nn**ing, etc.
> *out-SIT'* — outsi**tt**ing, etc.
> *un-FIT'* — unfi**tt**ed, etc.
> *be-FIT'* — befi**tt**ing, etc.

In the class of *out' fit* is a word like *wood' cut,* in which the accent is on *wood.* In actuality, however, we are dealing with the one-syllable verb *cut,* and so we disregard accent and write *woodcutter,* having doubled the final *t.*

That does it, so far.

We have added the concept of *accent* to the many other requirements of the doubling principle — and there is still one more qualification to learn.

This qualification will be discussed in Chapter 22, when we consider the concept of "accent shift." Eventually you will understand the doubling principle in all its multifarious aspects, with all its complicated qualifications and exceptions, with all its elaborate conditions.

Within a short time, you will have the doubling principle under such full control that you will automatically double or refrain from doubling without even thinking of the rule.

For note this about rules.

Rules, like mnemonics, are a means, not an end.

No one will ever ask you to quote a rule word for word —

And you have not, I hope, been making any attempt to memorize rules verbatim.

If you can quote the rule but you still misspell the word to which the rule applies, then, obviously, your approach is all wrong.

You are trying to learn rules instead of learning to spell.

Like a mnemonic, a rule has only one purpose —

And that is to *explain* a spelling, so that you can adjust intellectually to the correct pattern of letters and thus become visually and kinesthetically accustomed to it.

So that you can become so accustomed to the correct pattern that the rule fades from your conscious mind, but the unconscious visual and kinesthetic memories remain forever.

Learn spelling rules, and especially the complex doubling principle, not as a memory feat, but solely as a means of adjusting to the correct patterns of large groups of words.

In short, *understand* the rule and how it applies —

Do not attempt to memorize it.

TEST YOURSELF

Add the indicated suffix to each word. Note where the accent falls in each case before you decide whether or not to double the final consonant — and notice also whether the suffix to be added starts with a vowel or consonant.

1. ac-quit' + -*ed* _____ (acquitted)

2. ac-quit' + -*al* _____ (acquittal)

3. com-mit' + -*ed* _____ (committed)

4. com-mit' + -*ment* _____ (commitment)

5. ben'-efit + -*ed* _____ (benefited)

6. ben'-efit + -*ing* _____ (benefiting)

7. val'-et + -*ed* _____ (valeted)

8. a-bet' + -*ed* _____ (a-betted)

9. for-get' + -*ing* _____ (forgetting)

10. al-lot' + -*ed* _____ (allotted)

11. al-lot' + -*ment* _____ (allotment)

12. re-gret' + -*ed* _____ (regretted)

13. a-but' + -*ment* _____ (abutment)

14. ad-mit' + -*ing* _____ (admitting)

15. trans-mit' + -ed _____ (transmitted)

16. cov'-et + -ing _____ (coveting)

17. prof'-it + -er _____ (profiter)

18. com-mit' + -ee _____ (committee)

19. cor'-set + -ed _____ (corseted)

20. be-fit' + -ing _____ (befitting)

21. o-mit' + -ed _____ (omitted)

22. outwit' + -ed _____ (outwitted)

23. mis-be-got' + -en _____ (misbegotten)

24. wood'-cut + -er _____ (woodcutter)

25. mer'-it + -ed _____ (merited)

26. re-gret' + -ful _____ (regretful)

27. dis-com'-fit + -ure _____ (discomfiture)

28. in-hib'-it + -ion _____ (inhibition)

29. riv'-et + -ed _____ (riveted)

30. sub-mit' + -ed _____ (submitted)

31. un-fit' + -ed _____ (unfitted)

32. in-ter-mit' + -ent _____ (intermittent)

33. vis'-it + -or _____ (visitor)

34. cro-chet' + -ing _____ (crocheting)

35. cro-chet' + -ed _____ (crocheted)

36. ri-co-chet' + -ed _____ (ricocheted)

37. ri-co-chet' + -ing _____ (ricocheting)

38. prof'-it + -ed _____ (profited)

39. in-hib'-it + -ed _____ (inhibited)

40. pro-hib'-it + -ion _____ (prohibition)

41. per-mit' + -er _____ (permitter)

42. per-mit' + -ed _____ (permitted)

43. per-mit' + -ing _____ (permitting)

44. dis-com'-fit + -ed _____ (discomfited)

45. trans-mit' + -al _____ (transmittal)

46. riv'-et + -er _____ (riveter)

22

How a Shifting Accent May
Alter the Spelling

PROBLEM
occurence *or* occurrence?
deference *or* deferrence?
occuring *or* occurring?
defering *or* deferring?

SOLUTION
To complete our total understanding of the doubling principle, we wish to explore in this chapter words which end in the single consonant *r* —

Because in such words, almost exclusively, there enters the new factor of *accent shift*.

And *accent shift* will exercise an important influence on your decision to double a consonant or leave it alone.

Accent shift sounds like a scholarly and academic phrase — it is actually, however, quite easy to understand.

Let me illustrate.

Take *prefer*.

You will recognize it at once as a word that meets all the requirements so far detailed for the operation of the doubling principle.

Prefer ends in a single consonant (*r*) preceded by a single vowel (*e*).

Prefer is accented on the last syllable (*pre-FER'*).

If you decided to add a suffix which starts with a vowel (*-ed*, *-ing*, etc.) you would expect to double the *r*, producing *preferred*, *preferring*, etc.

154

And you would, of course, be absolutely right in doubling the r.

Note, now, that *prefer* has two syllables: *pre-fer'*.

The accent falls on the last syllable, on the *-fer*.

In *preferred* and *preferring*, the accent remains on the same syllable on which it fell in *pre-FER'*; *pre-FERD'*, *pre-FER'*-ing.

There has been no accent shift.

But suppose we add the ending *-ence* to *prefer*?

Do we double the final r or leave it alone?

Or suppose we add the ending *-able* or *-ential* to *prefer*?

Again, do we double the r or leave it alone?

As it happens, in these cases we leave it alone.

Point 33

When the accent *shifts* as a result of adding a suffix to a verb, you do not double the final consonant.

Note in the chart below how often *accent shift* occurs in verbs which end in a single r preceded by a single vowel. And in every instance in which such *accent shift* occurs, we do *not* double the r.

CHART I

Original Verb	*Form with Added Suffix*
(Single final consonant preceded by single vowel, accent on last syllable)	(Note that the accent shifts and the original final consonant is not doubled)
(*in-FER'*) infer	(*IN'-fer-once*) inference _____
	(*in-fer-EN'-sh'l*) inferential _____
(*re-FER'*) refer	(*REF'-er-ence*) reference _____
	(*REF'-er-EE'*) referee _____
	(*REF'-er-EN'-dum*) referendum _____
	(*REF'-er-ent*) referent _____
(*con-FER'*) confer	(*CON'-fer-ence*) conference _____
	(*CON'-fer-EE*) conferee _____

CHART I (*continued*)

Original Verb	*Form with Added Suffix*
(*de-FER'*) defer	(*DEF'-er-ence*) deference _____
	(*def-er-EN'-sh'l*) deferential _____
(*pre-FER'*) prefer	(*PREF'-er-ence*) preference _____
	(*PREF'-er-a-b'l*) preferable _____
	(*pref-er-EN'-sh'l*) preferential _____

The foregoing chart merits a few moments of careful study. As soon as you see what I'm driving at, you will understand the final factor in the doubling principle — namely, *that the accent must REMAIN on the original final syllable before you double that original final consonant.*

To make this factor even clearer, let me chart these same verbs in combination with their forms which require the doubled consonant — the forms, that is, in which the accent does *not* shift.

CHART II

Original Verb	*Form With Added Suffix*
(Accent on last syllable)	(No shift in accent)
(*in-FER'*) infer	(*in-FERD'*) inferred _____
	(*in-FER'-ing*) inferring _____
(*re-FER'*) refer	(*re-FERD'*) referred _____
	(*re-FER'-ing*) referring _____
(*con-FER'*) confer	(*con-FERD'*) conferred _____
	(*con-FER'-ing*) conferring _____
(*de-FER'*) defer	(*de-FERD'*) deferred _____
	(*de-FER'-ing*) deferring _____
(*pre-FER'*) prefer	(*pre-FERD'*) preferred _____
	(*pre-FER'-ing*) preferring _____

A little study will clearly show the contrast between the two charts.

In Chart I, the accent shifts when the suffix is added, *and the r is not doubled.*

In Chart II, the accent does *not* shift, i.e., it remains on the original last syllable, *and the r is doubled.*

Charts of course always look a little forbidding.

Don't let these two charts frighten you — they're simple to understand and contain the key to an important factor of the doubling principle.

Let me emphasize this factor by repeating —

Point 33

If a word complies with all other qualifications of the doubling principle, *but suffers a shift in accent when a suffix is added, the original final consonant is not doubled.*

That isn't too difficult — and with all the work you have devoted to analyzing, understanding, and becoming adjusted to the various factors of the doubling principle, you are ready now to see the total principle in all its explicit wording without getting lost in the somewhat complex phraseology.

THE TOTAL DOUBLING PRINCIPLE

Condition 1

If a word contains a single syllable and ends in *a single consonant* preceded by *a single vowel* —

(hop)

Condition 2

Or if it contains two or more syllables; ends in a single consonant preceded by a single vowel; *and is accented on the final syllable* —

(commit′, but *not* cov′et)

You double the final consonant before adding a suffix —

Condition 3

If the suffix begins with a vowel —

(hopping, committing, but coveting, commitment)

Condition 4

Provided the accent does *not* shift off the original final syllable.

(occur' —occur' rence; but prefer' —pref' erence)

And that's it — taking care of all possible variations and omitting, so far, only a few isolated exceptional cases, which, of course, need always to be reckoned with.

These isolated exceptional cases will be considered in a later chapter. But first the usual test of your learning.

TEST YOURSELF

Add the indicated suffix to each verb, remaining alert to whether the accent does or does not shift when the longer form is complete, and realizing, as always, that the doubling principle operates only if the suffix starts with a vowel.

1. infer' + -ed _____ (inferred)

2. prefer' + -ing _____ (preferring)

3. prefer' + -ence _____ (preference)

4. prefer' + -ential _____ (preferential)

5. prefer' + -ment _____ (preferment)

6. infer' + -ence _____ (inference)

7. refer' + -ed _____ (referred)

8. refer' + -ence _____ (reference)

9. refer' + -ent _____ (ref' erent)

10. confer' + -ing _____ (conferring)

11. confer' + -ence _____ (conference)

12. confer' + -ee _____ (conferee)

13. aver' + -ed _____ (averred)

14. bestir' + -ing _____ (bestirring)

15. defer' + -ment _____ (deferment)

16. defer' + -ence _____ (deference)

17. defer' + -ing _____ (deferring)

18. deter' + -ent _____ (deterrent)

19. deter' + -ence _____ (deterrence)

20. deter' + -ed _____ (deterred)

21. demur' + -al _____ (demurral)

22. demur' + -ed _____ (demurred)

23. incur' + -ence _____ (incurrence)

24. incur' + -ing _____ (incurring)

25. occur' + -ence _____ (occurrence)

26. occur' + -ing _____ (occurring)

27. recur' + -ence _____ (recurrence)

28. befur' + -ed _____ (befurred)

29. concur' + -ence _____ (concurrence)

30. inter' + -ed _____ (interred)

31. inter' + -ment _____ (interment)

32. occur' + -ed _____ (occurred)

23

A Quick New Look at the Doubling Principle

PROBLEMS

kidnaped *or* kidnapped?
counselor *or* counsellor?
development *or* developement?
developed *or* developped?

SOLUTION

We have covered now, with detailed thoroughness and in almost all possible contingencies, the principles that govern the doubling of final consonants when suffixes are added.

We explored, in Chapter 20, one-syllable words to which the doubling principle applies, and you learned:

— That if such words end in a single consonant preceded by a single vowel, you double that consonant before adding a suffix beginning with a vowel: bag — baggage, strip — stripping, etc.

— That important exceptional cases are gases, gaseous, gasify, etc., and the optional spelling buses.

In Chapter 21 we considered words of more than one syllable, and you learned:

— To be alert to the position of the accent, doubling when the accent falls on the final syllable (al-lot´ — al-lott´ed, per-mit´ — per-mitt´ing, etc.), but not when the accent falls on any other syllable (ben´e-fit — ben´e-fit-ing, prof´it — prof´it-ed, etc.).

160

We discussed, in Chapter 22, the influence of accent shifts, and you learned:

— To refrain from doubling if the accent *shifts off* the original final syllable (pre-fer´ — pref°er-ence, de-fer´ — def-er-en´tial).

— To double in the same words if the accent *does not* shift (pre-fer´ — pre-ferred´, de-fer´ — de-ferr´ing, occur´ — occurr´ence, etc.)

And now, because the doubling principle is the most complicated of all the rules of English spelling, but also one of the most valuable, far-reaching, and trustworthy, it will pay us to take a quick run-down on it, highlighting, for purposes of productive review, words of more than one syllable ending in consonants other than the two (namely *t* and *r*) on which we concentrated in previous pages.

I

We know that we double the final consonant of a word before adding a vowel suffix provided:

The original verb ended in a single consonant preceded by a single vowel —

The accent falls on the last syllable —

And the accent does not shift off that original last syllable in the longer form.

For example:

1. equip — equipped _____

       equipping _____ _____

2. reship — reshipping _____

       reshipped _____

3. begin — beginning _____

       beginner _____

4. control — controlled _____

       controlling _____

       controller _____

5. rebel — rebellious _____

   rebellion _____

   rebelled _____

   rebelling _____

6. excel — excelled _____

   excelling _____

7. patrol — patrolled _____

   patrolling _____

8. annul — annulled _____

   annulling _____

9. compel — compelling _____

   compelled _____

10. propel — propelling _____

    propelled _____

II

On the other hand, we know that we do not double the final consonant of words in which the accent falls on *other than the last syllable.* For example:

1. mur' mur — murmured, etc. _____

2. of' fer — offering, etc. _____

3. devel' op — devel' oping _____

   devel' oped _____

   devel' oper _____

4. gal' lop — gal' loping _____

   gal' loped _____

   gal' loper _____

5. wor' ship — wor' shiped _____

             wor' shiping _____

             wor' shiper _____

6. envel' op — envel' oped _____

             envel' oping _____

7. kid' nap — kid' naping _____

             kid' naped _____

             kid' naper _____

(Note the one *p* in all forms of *kidnap*. The double *p* in the longer forms is conventional British practice and occasionally found in American usage — but the regular single *p* form is preferred.)

8. impris' on — impris' oned, etc. _____

9. liv' en — livening, etc. _____

10. trav' el — trav' eler _____

             trav' eling _____

             trav' eled _____

11. can' cel — canceled _____

             can' celing _____

             can' celable _____

             can' celer _____

12. coun' sel — counseling _____

             coun' seled _____

             coun' selor _____

13. coun' cil — coun' cilor _____

14. sig' nal — sig' naling _____

             sig' naled _____

             sig' naler _____

15. shov'el — shov'eled _____

        shov'eler _____

        shov'eling _____

16. mar'vel — mar'velous _____

        mar'veled, etc. _____

(In examples 10–16, and in most other similar words ending in *l* and accented on the first syllable, the double *l* in the longer form is conventional British usage, and occasionally found in American writing. The single *l* form, however, is preferable and safer in this type of word.)

III

Let us now take, for the sake of complete clarity, overlearning, and thorough review, a final group of words which adhere to one of the qualifications of the doubling principle.

In the following forms the final consonant *is not doubled* because the suffix added starts with a *consonant,* not with a vowel.

1. equip + -ment = equipment _____

2. reship + -ment = reshipment _____

3. patrol + -man = patrolman _____

4. annul + -ment = annulment _____

5. develop + -ment = development _____

6. envelop + -ment = envelopment _____

7. worship + -ful = worshipful _____

(*Develop, envelop,* and *worship* would not double the *p* in any case, of course, since the accent does not fall on the last syllable — and the consonant at the beginning of the suffix is a kind of double insurance. Note that there is no *e* after the *p* in *development* or *envelopment,* though the use of the unnecessary *e* is a common and prevalent error. The verbs end in *p* and *-ment* is added — no need for inserting the *e.*)

If you fully understand the three charts around which this chapter is built, you are a master of the doubling principle. You can now make an immediate and accurate decision as to whether to double a final consonant or leave it alone — and you can make that decision with full assurance that you know both what you're doing and why you're doing it.

Unless, of course, you are dealing with an exceptional case.

We'll consider the important exceptions in the next chapter — but first, as usual,

TEST YOURSELF

Rewrite each word by adding the indicated suffix to the verb, remaining alert to the position of the accent and to whether the suffix starts with a vowel or consonant. Use, in all cases, the preferred American form.

I. Add -*ed*

1. equip′ _____ (equipped)

2. control′ _____ (controlled)

3. rebel′ _____ (rebelled)

4. excel′ _____ (excelled)

5. patrol′ _____ (patrolled)

6. annul′ _____ (annulled)

7. compel′ _____ (compelled)

8. propel′ _____ (propelled)

9. repel′ _____ (repelled)

10. impel′ _____ (impelled)

11. expel′ _____ (expelled)

12. dispel′ _____ (dispelled)

13. of′fer _____ (offered)

14. devel′op _____ (developed)

15. gal′lop _____ (galloped)

16. wal'lop _____ (walloped)

17. wor'ship _____ (worshiped)

18. envel'op _____ (enveloped)

19. kid'nap _____ (kidnaped)

20. trav'el _____ (traveled)

21. can'cel _____ (canceled)

22. coun'sel _____ (counseled)

23. sig'nal _____ (signaled)

24. shov'el _____ (shoveled)

25. mar'vel _____ (marveled)

II. Add -ing:

1. equip' _____ (equipping)

2. begin' _____ (beginning)

3. control' _____ (controlling)

4. rebel' _____ (rebelling)

5. excel' _____ (excelling)

6. patrol' _____ (patrolling)

7. annul' _____ (annulling)

8. compel' _____ (compelling)

9. repel' _____ (repelling)

10. impel' _____ (impelling)

11. expel' _____ (expelling)

12. dispel' _____ (dispelling)

13. dif'fer _____ (differing)

14. gal'lop _____ (galloping)

15. devel'op _____ (developing)

16. wal'lop _____ (walloping)

17. envel'op _____ (enveloping)

18. wor'ship _____ (worshiping)

19. kid'nap _____ (kidnaping)

20. rav'el _____ (raveling)

21. enam'el _____ (enameling)

22. coun'sel _____ (counseling)

23. trav'el _____ (traveling)

24. can'cel _____ (canceling)

25. grov'el _____ (groveling)

26. li'bel _____ (libeling)

III. Add *-er* or *-or*:

1. begin' _____ (beginner)

2. control' _____ (controller)

3. expel' _____ (expeller)

4. of'fer _____ (offerer)

5. devel'op _____ (developer)

6. wor'ship _____ (worshiper)

7. kid'nap _____ (kidnaper)

8. trav'el _____ (traveler)

9. coun'sel _____ (counselor)

10. coun'cil _____ (councilor)

11. sig'nal _____ (signaler)

12. jew'el _____ (jeweler)

13. grov'el _____ (groveler)

14. mod'el _____ (modeler)

15. shov'el _____ (shoveler)

IV. Add -*ment*:

1. equip _____ (equi**p**ment)

2. reship _____ (reshi**p**ment)

3. annul _____ (annu**l**ment)

4. develop _____ (develo**p**ment)

5. envelop _____ (envelo**p**ment)

A Footnote on Controller-Comptroller

If you have ever been intrigued, and possibly a little puzzled, by the spelling *comptroller,* you may be interested to learn that this pattern is now obsolete except as the title of the treasurer of a corporation or of a government organization; in which areas of American life adherence to tradition is sometimes so strong that modern usage has a hard time. It may very well be that *comptroller* seems more impressive and dignified than *controller,* but both words are pronounced identically (*kon-TROL-er*) and there is no rational need for the ancient and illogical spelling.

(Fourteenth Day, concluded)

PRETEST

1. pro**noun**ciation *or* pro**nun**ciation?
2. sacri**le**gious *or* sacre**li**gious?
3. gene**o**logy *or* genea**l**ogy?
4. miner**o**logy *or* minera**l**ogy?
5. main**tain**ance *or* main**ten**ance?

MNEMONICS

One thing you *cannot* bank on in English spelling: that if you can pronounce a word you can also spell it — correctly.

Spelling often enough follows pronunciation — just as often, especially in the troublesome words, it does not.

Take *victuals* — pronounced, of all things, *vittles.* Or *viscount,* pronounced *VYE-kount.* Or *phlegmatic,* in which the *g* is sounded, and *phlegm,* in which it is silent. Or *column,* in which the *n* is silent, and *columnist,* in which it is sounded.

Or, of course, the famous *-ough* combinations —

> pronounced OFF, in *cough*
> pronounced OO, in *through*
> pronounced O, in *though*
> pronounced OU, in *bough*
> pronounced UFF, in *rough*

And so on, without end.

However, there are a number of demons which *can* be spelled correctly if pronounced carefully. Five such demons are the words in the pretest of this chapter — all of which have the common mnemonic of careful pronunciation.

1. (pro**noun**ciation *or* pro**nun**ciation?)

Be alert when you come to the second syllable of this word — which is pronounced and spelled *nun.*

Correct Spelling: pro**nun**ciation _____

Mnemonic: pro-**NUN**-ci-a-tion

2. (sacrilegious *or* sacreligious?)

In the preferable form of this word, the second syllable is pronounced *ri* (as in *rim*), the following syllable *ee* (as in *legal*); suiting spelling to sound, we write SAC-R**I**-LE-GIOUS. Do not confuse SACR**IL**EGIOUS with *religious;* the two words are sharply dissimilar in meaning and have an opposite combination of the vowels *i* and *e*.

The noun from SACR**IL**EGIOUS has the pattern you would expect: SACR**IL**EGE.

Correct Spelling: sacrilegious _____

Mnemonic: sac-ri-**LE**-gious

3. (geneology *or* genealogy?)

Most such words (and there are hundreds of them) do end in *-ology* — this is one of the three common ones which end in *-alogy*. Pronounce and spell it ge-ne-**AL**-o-gy;

Correct Spelling: genealogy _____

Mnemonic: ge-ne-**AL**-o-gy

4. (minerology *or* mineralogy?)

And MINER**A**LOGY is the second of the three common words which end in *-alogy*. Pronounce and spell it min-er-**AL**-o-gy. (The third word is *analogy*, usually pronounced and spelled without error.) Note also that MINER**A**LOGY comes from MINER**A**L.

Correct Spelling: mineralogy _____

Mnemonic: min-er-**AL**-o-gy

5. (maintainance *or* maintenance?)

Although the verb is *maintain*, pronounced as spelled, the noun form changes *-tain* to *-ten*, and is pronounced accordingly: MAIN-**ten**-ance. This is similar, as you notice, to the change from PRO-**NOUN**CE to PRO**NUN**CIATION.

Correct Spelling: main**ten**ance _____

Mnemonic: MAIN-**ten**-ance

MNEMONICS CHART

Correct Pattern	Mnemonic
1. pro**nun**ciation	pro-**NUN**-ci-a-tion
2. sacri**le**gious	sac-ri-**LE**-gious
3. gene**al**ogy	ge-ne-**AL**-o-gy
4. miner**al**ogy	min-er-**AL**-o-gy
5. main**ten**ance	MAIN-**ten**-ance

TEST YOURSELF

I. Check the correct pattern.

1. (a) minerology,   (b) mineralogy   (b)
2. (a) sacrilegious,   (b) sacreligious   (a)
3. (a) pronounciation, (b) pronunciation   (b)
4. (a) maintenance,   (b) maintainance   (a)
5. (a) geneology,   (b) genealogy   (b)

II. Recall the mnemonic for each word.

1. accelerate _____ (celerity)

2. occurrence _____ (current event)

3. anoint _____ (**an oil**)

4. devise _____ (devious)

5. superintendent _____ (**rent**)

6. iridescent _____ (iris)

7. inoculate _____ (inject)

8. tranquillity _____ (**quill**)

9. grammar _____ (**mar**)

10. indispensable _____ (**able** worker)

III. Decide on the crucial missing letter or letters, then rewrite the complete word.

1. miner — logy _____ (a)

2. maint — nance _____ (e)

3. pron — nciation _____ (u)

4. sacr — l — gious _____ (i,e)

5. gene — logy _____ (a)

6. i — o — ulate _____ (n,c)

7. indispens — ble _____ (a)

8. superintend — nt _____ (e)

9. tranqui — ity _____ (ll)

10. i — idescent _____ (r)

11. gramm — r _____ (a)

12. occu — nce _____ (rre)

13. d — vise _____ (e)

14. acce — erate _____ (l)

15. a — oint _____ (n)

24

How to Handle Real and Apparent Violations of the Doubling Principle

PROBLEMS
 combating *or* comba**tt**ing?
 crystalize *or* crystallize?
 canva**s**es *or* canva**ss**es?
 chagri**n**ed *or* chagri**nn**ed?

SOLUTION

Now that you are a master of the doubling principle —

Now that you are familiar and at ease with all its complex provisions —

Now that you can handle, without hesitation, every *regular* doubling problem that can possibly occur —

You are ready to study some of the *irregular* problems, those plaguing and perplexing exceptional cases which are likely to cause confusion.

These exceptional cases, in most instances, have neither rhyme nor reason (but where any helpful reasons exist, I'll pass them along to you), and you will simply have to accept them as rebels or misfits, relying strongly on your visual memory and on the fact that exceptions somehow manage to stick in the mind with no great effort. These are blocks that we can't comfortably fit into the general structure of the doubling principle — so we'll let them stand out conspicuously.

Exceptional Case 1

Can' cel, chan' cel, crys' tal, met' al, and *tran' quil* are, as you can see, accented on the first syllable rather than the last syllable.

173

By the provisions of the doubling principle, therefore, we should not double the final consonant before adding a vowel suffix — *canceled, canceling, metaled*, etc.

Nevertheless, in the following, and only the following, *exceptional forms*, we *do* double the final *l*. These are exceptions to the doubling principle and should be learned as such.

1. cancellation _____		5. crystalline _____	
2. chancellery _____		6. metallic _____	
3. chancellor _____		7. metallurgy _____	
4. crystallize _____		8. tranquillity _____	

Exceptional Case 2

Excel is accented on the last syllable — hence we write *excelled* and *excelling*. In *excellent* and *excellence* the accent shifts and, by a provision of the doubling principle, only one *l* should be required. Nevertheless, the only correct forms contain double *l*'s.

9. excellent _____   10. excellence _____

Exceptional Case 3

Chagrin (pronounced *sha-GRIN*) is accented on the last syllable — we should therefore double final *n* before adding a vowel suffix. But we don't. The only correct patterns, strange as they may look, are:

11. chagrining _____   12. chagrined _____

Exceptional Case 4

Handicap is accented on the first syllable — by the doubling principle we would not expect to double the final *p*. However, we do.

13. handicapping _____   15. handicapper _____

14. handicapped _____

The reason for this anomaly is the fact that the word is a combination of *cap* plus *handy* — and we treat it as a one-syllable verb, following the analogy of *capping, capper*, etc. We react similarly to other verbs which are made up of two words, even though the

accent does not occur on the last syllable — for example *horse'-whip, o'verstep, weath'erstrip, eaves'drop, o'vertip,* etc.
Thus:

16. horsewhipped, _____
    etc.
17. overstepping, _____
    etc.
18. weatherstripped, _____
    etc.

19. eavesdropping, _____
    etc.
20. overtipper, _____
    etc.

And we have the same reaction also to *hum'bug* and *zig'zag.* Accent is on the first syllable, but we are influenced by the words *bug* and *zag,* and so we write only:

21. humbugged _____
22. humbugging _____

23. zigzagged _____
24. zigzagging _____

(Apparently) Exceptional Case 5

Bias and *focus* (pronounced *BYE-'ss, FO-k'ss*) are accented on the first rather than the last syllable. By the doubling principle, therefore, we should *not* double final *s,* and you will be happy to hear that in America it is preferred usage not to.

25. biases _____
26. biased _____
27. biasing _____

28. focuses _____
29. focused _____
30. focusing _____

You may therefore be confused by these correct spellings:

31. canvasses _____
32. canvassed _____

33. canvassing _____
34. canvasser _____

Especially when you know that the accent in each instance is on the first syllable only.

As soon as you realize the parent verb from which forms 31–34 come, your confusion will vanish. The original verb is *canvass,* not *canvas.* Note the double *s* in the original verb and you will understand the double *s* in the longer, derived forms. *Canvass,* ending not in a single consonant but in double *s,* does not operate under the doubling principle.

But what about *canvas*?

Canvas (one *s*) is a noun only, meaning either a kind of cloth or a painting. It has a plural *canvases*, but should not be confused with the verb to *canvass*, which in all forms contains the double *s*.

(*Apparently*) *Exceptional Case 6*

The verb *to combat* may cause considerable confusion.

Originally (and up to about ten years ago) practically the only pronunciation heard from educated speakers was COM'bat, accent on the first syllable.

But, especially lately, the verb has been receiving a second-syllable accent (com-BAT'), not only on the popular level but also from large groups of cultivated speakers — and is thus sanctioned by modern dictionaries.

Which makes for a dilemma.

Do we suit the spelling of the longer forms of *combat* to the original, or to the newer and increasingly popular, pronunciation?

That is, do we double the *t* when we add the suffixes *-ed*, *-er*, *-ive*, *-ant*, and *-ing*, as we do in other verbs like *per-MIT'*, *com-MIT'*, etc., that are accented on the last syllable?

Or do we leave the *t* alone?

You will find the answer in this principle of English spelling:

Words rarely change their spelling no matter how radically the pronunciation changes.

So pronounce *combat* and its various forms in whatever way you like, with the accent either on the *com-* or on the *-bat* — but spell it as if the accent were always on the first syllable.

Thus:

35. combated _____   38. combater _____

36. combating _____   39. combative _____

37. combatant _____

Never a double *t* in any form of *combat*, no matter what pronunciation you habitually use and feel comfortable with.

Our six exceptional (or apparently exceptional) cases drive the final nail into our construction of the complete doubling principle — all possible aspects and important exceptions are now accounted for and hammered into place. No form of any verb can possibly be a matter of doubt once you completely understand every facet of, and exception to, this valuable principle.

Here, once again, are the thirty-nine words discussed in this chapter — become visually and kinesthetically familiar with them before you test your learning.

1. cancellation _____	21. humbugged _____
2. chancellery _____	22. humbugging _____
3. chancellor _____	23. zigzagged _____
4. crystallize _____	24. zigzagging _____
5. crystalline _____	25. biases _____
6. metallic _____	26. biased _____
7. metallurgy _____	27. biasing _____
8. tranquillity _____	28. focuses _____
9. excellent _____	29. focused _____
10. excellence _____	30. focusing _____
11. chagrining _____	31. canvasses _____
12. chagrined _____	32. canvassed _____
13. handicapping _____	33. canvassing _____
14. handicapped _____	34. canvasser _____
15. handicapper _____	35. combated _____
16. horsewhipped _____	36. combating _____
17. overstepping _____	37. combatant _____
18. weatherstripped _____	38. combater _____
19. eavesdropping _____	39. combative _____
20. overtipper _____	

TEST YOURSELF

Rewrite the following words with the indicated suffix.

1. cancel + *-ation* _____ (cancellation)

2. excel + *-ency* _____ (excellency)

3. crystal + *-ize* _____ (crystallize)

4. metal + *-urgy* _____ (metallurgy)

5. tranquil + *-ity* _____ (tranquillity)

6. chagrin + *-ed* _____ (chagrined)

7. chagrin + *-ing* _____ (chagrining)

8. chancel + *-ery* _____ (chancellery)

9. chancel + *-or* _____ (chancellor)

10. crystal + *-ine* _____ (crystalline)

11. metal + *-ic* _____ (metallic)

12. handicap + *-ed* _____ (handicapped)

13. eavesdrop + *-ed* _____ (eavesdropped)

14. humbug + *-ed* _____ (humbugged)

15. bias + *-ed* _____ (biased)

16. focus + *-ed* _____ (focused)

17. canvass + *-ed* _____ (canvassed)

18. combat + *-ed* _____ (combated)

19. combat + *-ing* _____ (combating)

20. combat + *-ive* _____ (combative)

A Note to the Overconscientious

You can make the acquisition of a high degree of skill in spelling a monotonous and needlessly difficult task — if you wish to.

You can accomplish this negative feat by strict and careful memorizing of the principles with which these pages deal, so that you can reel them off word by word.

If you manage finally to spout such verbatim reports of the spelling principles, you are learning rules, not spelling.

For spelling deals with individual words, not with general rules — and one facet of skill in spelling is an instantaneous and accurate reaction to a word by what we might call "successful grouping."

Which means that you recognize, from an *understanding* of principles, that a word belongs in a certain category. For example, if called upon to write *analyze,* you recall it automatically as a member of the *analyze-paralyze* group, as one of the only two common words ending in *-yze.*

For example, if called upon to write *proceed,* you recall it automatically as one of the only three *-ceed* words in the language (*succeed, proceed, exceed*).

For example, if called upon to write *insistent,* you recall it automatically as one of the *rent* words — *insistent, persistent, superintendent, dependent.*

For example, if called upon to write *occurred,* you recall it automatically as one of the doubling words in which the accent remains on the original final syllable, a member of the *referred-preferred-incurred-inferred-* etc. group.

For example, if called upon to write *combated,* you recall it automatically as a form of one of the verbs in which the accent does not fall on the last syllable, despite its popular pronunciation. Or you recall *chagrined* as one of the exceptional cases under the doubling principle.

And so on.

Such ability to group a word successfully comes not from monotonously memorizing principles —

But rather, and most efficiently, from thoroughly *understanding* the provisions of, exceptions to, and, where they exist, the reasons for, the principles that govern correct patterns.

Plus (and this is most important) constant *kinesthetic* and *visual* practice with all the individual words that occur under each principle.

As to this complicated and important doubling principle with which we have been working so carefully for the last few chapters — I beg you, make no attempt to memorize it to the point where you can repeat it verbatim.

Instead, bend your efforts to a full and active *understanding* of its provisions and exceptions. Become visually and kinesthetically adjusted to the individual words which the principle governs. And shortly, though the principle and all its complex phraseology may vanish from your conscious mind, there will be a residue of result which will make your spelling error-free on all words considered in these chapters.

In this way you will completely avoid the monotonous and needlessly difficult aspects of spelling — and become a perfect, or near-perfect, speller through active learning and stimulating experiences.

Third Review

Your training program is now three fourths complete —

And if you have been working intensively and conscientiously, you have developed to a high degree your visual and kinesthetic memory of the correct patterns of hundreds and hundreds of commonly misspelled words; you have made a healthy intellectual adjustment to a number of very important basic principles in English spelling.

Let us now review your grasp of the material in Chapters 18–24 and your ability to respond accurately with the proper patterns of the words discussed.

BASIC PRINCIPLES

1. The choice between -cy and -sy, or between -ence and -ense, will not be troublesome except in the following important words:

1. defense _____   6. idiosyncrasy _____

2. offense _____   7. apostasy _____

3. pretense _____   8. hypocrisy _____

4. license _____   9. to prophesy _____

5. ecstasy _____   (the verb)

2. Similarly, in most words which allow a logical choice between -ify and -efy, the probable ending is -ify. But four words end in -efy only:

1. liquefy _____   3. stupefy _____

2. rarefy _____   4. putrefy _____

181

3. One-syllable words ending in a single consonant preceded by a single vowel double that final consonant before adding a vowel suffix:

(quiz) quizzes _____ (trip) tripping _____
                                      etc.

4. Exceptions are:

(gas) gases _____ (bus) buses _____

  gaseous _____   (*busses* equally acceptable)

  gasify _____   etc.

5. But *gassed* and *gassing* are not exceptions.

6. If a word contains more than one syllable, and the accent falls on the final syllable, with all other conditions of the doubling principle operating,[1] the final consonant is doubled — provided the addition of the suffix does not cause the accent to shift.

(allot) allotted _____ (commit) committed _____
                                      etc.

7. But if the accent falls on any but the final syllable, the final consonant is *not* doubled:

(benefit) benefited _____ (profit) profiting _____
                                      etc.

8. If a word ends in -*et* pronounced *ay*, the final consonant is *not* doubled when a suffix is added.

ricocheted _____ crocheted _____
                                      etc.

9. Certain verbs made up of two separate parts are treated as one-syllable words — the final ~~accent~~ *consonant* is therefore doubled no matter where the accent falls.

outfitted _____ woodcutter _____
                                      etc.

[1]Single consonant preceded by a single vowel, suffix starting with a vowel.

10. Even though a verb meets all the conditions of the doubling principle, if the addition of a suffix shifts the accent *off* the *original last syllable* the final consonant is *not* doubled. Most such examples end in r.

(defer) deference _____ (prefer) preference _____

etc.

11. The following important forms, among others (as explained in Chapter 24), are exceptional cases:

cancellation _____   chagrining _____

chancellery _____   chagrined _____

chancellor _____   handicapping _____

crystallize _____   canvassing _____

metallic _____   combated _____

metallurgy _____   combatant _____

tranquillity _____   combative _____

excellent _____   combating _____

excellence _____

THIRD REVIEW TEST

I. Add either -cy or -sy to the following, rewriting the complete word.

  1. idiosyncra — _____ (sy)

  2. a prophe — _____ (cy)
     (noun)

  3. to prophe — _____ (sy)
     (verb)

  4. ecsta — _____ (sy)

  5. vacan — _____ (cy)

  6. pleuri — _____ (sy)

  7. courte — _____ (sy)

8. pira — _____ (cy)

9. aposta — _____ (sy)

10. fanta — _____ (sy)

11. suprema — _____ (cy)

II. Add either *-efy* or *-ify* to the following, rewriting the complete word.

1. class — _____ (ify)

2. liqu — _____ (efy)

3. cert — _____ (ify)

4. rar — _____ (efy)

5. pac — _____ (ify)

6. stup — _____ (efy)

7. putr — _____ (efy)

8. rat — _____ (ify)

III. Add the indicated ending to each word, rewriting in its complete form.

1. gas + *-es* _____ (ga**s**es)

2. bus + *-es* _____ (bu**s**es or (bu**ss**es)

3. gas + *-eous* _____ (ga**s**eous)

4. gas + *-ify* _____ (ga**s**ify)

5. gas + *-ed* _____ (ga**ss**ed)

6. gas + *-ing* _____ (ga**ss**ing)

7. quiz + *-es* _____ (qui**zz**es)

8. quiz + *-ing* _____ (qui**zz**ing)

9. quit + *-ing* _____ (qui**tt**ing)

10. ship + *-ing* _____ (shi**pp**ing)

11. ship + *-ment* _____ (shi**p**ment)

12. scar + -*ed* _____ (scarred)

13. begin + -*ing* _____ (beginning)

14. allot + -*ed* _____ (allotted)

15. allot + -*ment* _____ (allotment)

16. benefit + -*ed* _____ (benefited)

17. acquit + -*ed* _____ (acquitted)

18. commit + -*ing* _____ (committing)

19. transmit + -*al* _____ (transmittal)

20. regret + -*able* _____ (regrettable)

21. banquet + -*ed* _____ (banqueted)

22. crochet + -*ed* _____ (crocheted)

23. occur + -*ing* _____ (occurring)

24. occur + -*ence* _____ (occurrence)

25. defer + -*ing* _____ (deferring)

26. defer + -*ence* _____ (deference)

27. refer + -*ed* _____ (referred)

28. refer + -*ence* _____ (reference)

29. deter + -*ence* _____ (deterrence)

30. abhor + -*ent* _____ (abhorrent)

31. concur + -*ence* _____ (concurrence)

32. demur + -*al* _____ (demurral)

33. kidnap + -*er* _____ (kidnaper)

34. counsel + -*ed* _____ (counseled)

35. rebel + -*ing* _____ (rebelling)

36. travel + -*ing* _____ (traveling)

37. develop + -*ed* _____ (developed)

38. equip + -*ment* _____   (equipment)

39. develop + -*ment* _____   (development)

40. cancel + -*ation* _____   (cancellation)

41. metal + -*urgy* _____   (metallurgy)

42. tranquil + -*ity* _____   (tranquillity)

43. tranquil + -*ize* _____   (tranquilize)

44. chagrin + -*ing* _____   (chagrining)

45. combat + -*ing* _____   (combating)

46. bias + -*ed* _____   (biased)

How to Decide Between -ence and -ance

PROBLEMS
   refe**rence** *or* refe**rance**?
   resist**ence** *or* resist**ance**?
   abho**rrance** *or* abho**rrence**?
   persever**ance** *or* persever**ence**?

SOLUTION
   Probably the one all-inclusive reason why English spelling seems so illogical and frustrating is that, by the very nature of our language, almost every word in it has come from some foreign tongue.

   The great base on which English rests is Anglo-Saxon, which is a combination of *German* dialects.

   With the Roman invasion of Britain in early times, followed by Danish and Norman (French) conquerors, our language began to develop along *Latin, Scandinavian,* and *French* lines.

   And then, with the revival of learning after the Middle Ages, great numbers of *Latin* and *Greek* terms and roots were used for building the rapidly increasing English vocabulary.

   In addition to all of which, English is a thieving kind of language, and has always borrowed flagrantly from *every civilized tongue* and from many primitive ones.

   With the result that 95 per cent of our vocabulary has some kind of foreign background.

   And, in most cases, though we give a word an Anglicized pronunciation, we faithfully follow the foreign spelling.

   It is the foreign spelling that accounts for the middle s of *supersede* (Latin *sedeo,* to sit) —

   For the *ph* instead of *f* in words like *telephone, phonetic, symphony,* etc. (all from Greek *phone,* sound).

187

For the illogical double *t* in *dilettante*[1] (Italian *dilettare*, to delight).

For the illogical double *c* in *desiccate*[2] (Latin *siccus*, dry).

For the -*sy* ending of *ecstasy* (old French *extasie*).

And so on, indefinitely.

It is the foreign derivation which in the main accounts for the endings -ence and -ance.

Which puts Americans without a thorough classical education behind that well-known eight-ball when it comes to deciding whether to end a word with -*ence* or -*ance*.

There is, as it happens, a kind of uniform principle governing the distinction between these endings.

And that is — if the English word ultimately derives from a "first conjugation" Latin verb, the ending is generally -*ance*.

But if the English word ultimately derives from a Latin verb of any other "conjugation," the ending is generally -*ence*.

Which, is, I fully and sympathetically admit, no help to you whatever.

For there is no way, unless you are, or have been, a Latin scholar, to determine the "conjugation" of the Latin origin of an English word.

And, in addition, with one minor exception to be noted shortly, there is no other uniform principle (beyond this knowledge of Latin verbs) which will help you make an accurate choice between -*ence* and -*ance*.

In this type of problem you will have to rely almost exclusively on developing your visual and kinesthetic responsiveness to a very high degree.

Let us first consider the minor exception.

Which is, that every English verb ending in *r*, preceded by a single vowel, and accented on the last syllable, forms its noun with -*ence*.

We are already quite familiar with this type of verb, having considered it exhaustively in Chapter 22, in which we studied *accent shifts*.

---

[1] One who dabbles in the fine arts.

[2] To dry up. Weird as the proper pattern of this obscure word may look, it is correct only with one *s*, two *c*'s.

Here, for example, is a fairly complete list.

VERB	NOUN	
1. in-fer′	inference	_____
2. pre-fer′	preference	_____
3. in-cur′	incurrence	_____
4. oc-cur′	occurrence	_____
5. re-fer′	reference	_____
6. trans-fer′	transference	_____
7. de-ter′	deterrence	_____
8. re-cur′	recurrence	_____
9. con-cur′	concurrence	_____
10. ab-hor′	abhorrence	_____
11. con-fer′	conference	_____
12. de-fer′	deference	_____

On this much, then, you can rely — if the verb is one of the type we have studied in Chapter 22, the noun will definitely end in -*ence* only.

But that's just about as far as we can go with any assurance.

From this point on, you can begin to master the -*ence* — -*ance* problem only by taking two consecutive steps.

Step 1

Determine by the tests that follow which of the commonly confusing -*ence* — -*ance* forms leave you in a dilemma.

Step 2

Concentrate on these personally perplexing nouns, developing, through practice, a keen visual and kinesthetic responsiveness to the correct ending.

Let us see how these steps work out and how effectively they operate for your type of difficulty.

TEST I

Complete these twenty words with either *-ance* or *-ence*, whichever you trust. If in serious doubt, leave the answer blank.

1. admitt — _____
2. adher — _____
3. compet — _____
4. deliver — _____
5. confid — _____
6. depend — _____
7. persist — _____
8. diffid — _____
9. opul — _____
10. assur — _____

11. repent — _____
12. toler — _____
13. preval — _____
14. attend — _____
15. preced — _____
16. extravag — _____
17. rever — _____
18. coher — _____
19. subsist — _____
20. exist — _____

Key to Test 1:

Check your responses against the correct endings below. Where you made an error or left an answer blank, commit the pattern to visual memory and write the correct spelling in the appropriate blank.

1. admitt**ance** _____
2. adher**ence** _____
3. compet**ence** _____
4. deliver**ance** _____
5. confid**ence** _____
6. depend**ence** _____
7. persist**ence** _____
8. diffid**ence** _____
9. opul**ence** _____
10. assur**ance** _____

11. repent**ance** _____
12. toler**ance** _____
13. preval**ence** _____
14. attend**ance** _____
15. preced**ence** _____
16. extravag**ance** _____
17. rever**ence** _____
18. coher**ence** _____
19. subsist**ence** _____
20. exist**ence** _____

The probability is that you made only a few errors, left only a few blanks. For most people, by some strange alchemy, do not have too much trouble with the *-ance —-ence* endings, somehow developing, through years of reading and writing, an accurate "feel" for the required ending.

But tighten up your reaction to those errors you did make. Study once again whatever forms caused you trouble, gaining a strong and lasting visual impression.

After you have done that, circle below the numbers of the words on which you erred, and attempt to fill in the correct endings of the circled words. To check your learning, refer again to the key to Test I, above.

RETEST I

1. admitt _____	11. repent _____
2. adher _____	12. toler _____
3. compet _____	13. preval _____
4. deliver _____	14. attend _____
5. confid _____	15. preced _____
6. depend _____	16. extravag _____
7. persist _____	17. rever _____
8. diffid _____	18. coher _____
9. opul _____	19. subsist _____
10. assur _____	20. exist _____

With some degree of success behind you, you are ready to repeat your training, step by step, on a second group of twenty commonly confusing words.

TEST 2

1. susten _____	4. insist _____
2. differ _____	5. contriv _____
3. pertin _____	6. mainten _____

7. observ _____
8. superintend _____
9. abund _____
10. continu _____
11. resist _____
12. forbear _____
13. appurten _____

14. afflu _____
15. arrog _____
16. protuber _____
17. persever _____
18. relev _____
19. suffer _____
20. petul _____

Key to Test 2

1. susten**ance** _____
2. differ**ence** _____
3. pertin**ence** _____
4. insist**ence** _____
5. contriv**ance** _____
6. mainten**ance** _____
7. observ**ance** _____
8. superintend**ence** _____
9. abund**ance** _____
10. continu**ance** _____

11. resist**ance** _____
12. forbear**ance** _____
13. appurten**ance** _____
14. afflu**ence** _____
15. arrog**ance** _____
16. protuber**ance** _____
17. persever**ance** _____
18. relev**ance** _____
19. suffer**ance** _____
20. petul**ance** _____

RETEST 2

1. susten _____
2. differ _____
3. pertin _____
4. insist _____
5. contriv _____
6. mainten _____
7. observ _____

8. superintend _____
9. abund _____
10. continu _____
11. resist _____
12. forbear _____
13. appurten _____
14. afflu _____

15. arrog _____   18. (ir)relev _____

16. protuber _____   19. suffer _____

17. persever _____   20. petul _____

(Needless to say, if a noun ends in -*ence*, the adjective form similarly ends in -*ent*; and an -*ance* noun likewise has an -*ant* adjective. There is no exception to this principle.)

If you have found that -*ance*——-*ence* confusion is one of your spelling weaknesses, try these final exercises in which the forty troublesome words have been separated into two special groups — those that end in -*ance* and those that end in -*ence*. Take this further opportunity to tighten up your *visual* and *kinesthetic* reactions to each category, at the same time developing an *intellectual* awareness of the grouping to which each word belongs. As in all these exercises, use the window of the visual-aid card to examine the correct pattern for a few seconds, then write the word in the blank provided for that purpose.

Group I —— -*ance* Forms

1. admitt**ance** _____   12. continu**ance** _____

2. deliver**ance** _____   13. resist**ance** _____

3. assur**ance** _____   14. forbear**ance** _____

4. repent**ance** _____   15. appurten**ance** _____

5. toler**ance** _____   16. annoy**ance** _____

6. attend**ance** _____   17. protuber**ance** _____

7. extravag**ance** _____   18. persever**ance** _____

8. susten**ance** _____   19. (ir)relev**ance** _____

9. contriv**ance** _____   20. suffer**ance** _____

10. observ**ance** _____   21. petul**ance** _____

11. abund**ance** _____   22. mainten**ance** _____

Group II —— -*ence* Forms

1. adher**ence** _____   3. confid**ence** _____

2. compet**ence** _____   4. depend**ence** _____

5. persist**ence** _____   12. subsist**ence** _____

6. diffid**ence** _____   13. exist**ence** _____

7. opul**ence** _____   14. differ**ence** _____

8. preval**ence** _____   15. pertin**ence** _____

9. preced**ence** _____   16. insist**ence** _____

10. rever**ence** _____   17. superintend**ence** _____

11. coher**ence** _____   18. afflu**ence** _____.

You have tested yourself on, and begun to master by means of visual, kinesthetic and intellectual attack, forty of the most confusing *-ance — -ence* forms.

When you have these forty words under some measure of control —
Plus the twelve *-ence* forms on page 190 —
Then you have the fifty-two crucial possibilities of error licked.

Errors are rarely made on any of the other *-ence — -ance* forms, but if you should ever find yourself in doubt on some word other than one of the fifty-two covered in this chapter —
Work from the law of mathematical probability.

There are far more words ending in *-ence* than in *-ance.*

So, by the law of mathematical probability, you will be reasonably safe in ending the doubtful word with *-ence.*

And let us recall the opening principle of the chapter.

Point 34

Verbs ending in *r*, preceded by a single vowel, and accented on the last syllable, form nouns ending in *-ence* only.

A Footnote to Latin Scholars

(The next paragraph will have meaning for you only if you have studied Latin.)

If you are well acquainted with Latin verbs, you can often rely on the conjugation of the verb to disclose the choice between *-ence* and *-ance.* First conjugation verbs form English nouns ending in *-ance;* second, third, and fourth conjugation verbs form English nouns ending in *-ence.* This rule is not foolproof (*resistere*, for example, produces *resistance*) but works often enough to be useful.

A Footnote to All Readers

With this preliminary visual practice in *-ence* — *-ance* forms, you will notice that your eye will be arrested by almost every *-ence* — *-ance* word you meet in your reading. Do not resist the temptation to linger visually for a few seconds on these words. Such an activity will considerably increase your mastery of all *-ence* — *-ance* nouns, tremendously increase your assurance that you can quickly and successfully make the proper choice when the occasion requires.

MNEMONICS
Nine

PRETEST
1. descend**ent** *or* descend**ant**?
2. inimit**ible** *or* inimit**able**?
3. irrit**ible** *or* irrit**able**?
4. irresist**able** *or* irresist**ible**?
5. vilify *or* villify?

MNEMONICS
1. (descend**ent** *or* descend**ant**?)
A DESCEND**ANT** is a child, a grandchild, etc. As such he must have an **AN**CESTOR — and the vowel in the first syllable of **AN**-CESTOR is of course the key to the puzzling vowel of the last syllable in DESCEND**ANT**.

   Correct Spelling: descend**ant** _____

   Mnemonic:　　　**an**cestor

2. (inimit**ible** *or* inimit**able**?)
Relying on our most useful mnemonic, the linking up of a puzzling spelling to some form of the same word that is easy to spell, the obvious association for the adjective INIMIT**A**BLE is its allied verb form IMIT**A**TE — in both cases the vowel after the *t* is *a*.

   Correct Spelling: inimit**able** _____

   Mnemonic:　　　imit**a**te

3. (irrit**ible** *or* irrit**able**?)
And for this word we link the adjective form to the verb IRRIT**A**TE again the vowel *a* after the *t*.

   Correct Spelling: irrit**able** _____

   Mnemonic:　　　irrit**a**te

196

4. (irresis**table** *or* irresis**tible**?)

Contradictions abound in English spelling, as you know —
For example:
RESIST**ANCE** ends in -*ance* —
But IRRESIST**IBLE** and its less common affirmative form, RE-
SIST**IBLE**, do not end in -*able*, but in -*ible*.

This is similar to the contradiction you may recall in DEPEND-
ABLE-DEPEND**ENCE**, and is a fairly rare phenomenon, most -*ance*
words having the expected -*able* forms, -*ence* words having -*ible*
forms.

There are two danger spots in IRR**E**SIST**I**BLE — the fourth and
ninth letters, both of which are printed in heavy type. Most common
misspelling occurs on the ninth letter, for which an effective mnemonic is L**I**PST**I**CK. Women, let us say, consider that L**I**PST**I**CK
helps make them IRRESIST**I**BLE — and as the letter *i* is the only
vowel in L**I**PST**I**CK, you will know to use the -*ible* rather than the
-*able* ending.

There is a somewhat weaker tendency, among inefficient spellers,
to pattern IRR**E**SIST**I**BLE very much according to sound, especially
in the first two syllables, writing *irrisis*-. To avoid such confusion,
realize that you are working from the root R**E**SIST (which no one
misspells), plus the negative prefix *ir-*, plus the correct ending
-*ible* — result: IR-R**E**SIST-**I**BLE.

(A full exploration of the basic rules that govern all -*able* —
-*ible* words will be made in Chapters 28 and 29.)

> *Correct Spellings:* irresistible _____
>
> resistible _____
>
> *Mnemonic:* lipstick, resist

5. (vilify *or* villify?)

This word is accented on the first syllable; it is therefore no
wonder that many unsuspecting citizens are seduced into doubling
the *l*. However, only one *l* is permitted, owing to its derivation
from Latin *vilis*, *vile*. To VIL**I**FY is to speak evil of, to render
VI**LE** — and the related word VI**LE**, with one *l*, is the obvious
mnemonic.

> *Correct Spelling:* vilify _____
>
> *Mnemonic:* vile

TEST YOURSELF

I. Check the correct pattern.
   1. (a) descendent, (b) descendant   (b)
   2. (a) inimitible,   (b) inimitable   (b)
   3. (a) irritible,   (b) irritable   (b)
   4. (a) irresistible, (b) irresistable   (a)
   5. (a) vilify,   (b) villify   (a)

II. Recall the mnemonic for each word.

   1. vilify _____   (vile)

   2. irritable _____   (irritate)

   3. irresistible _____   (lipstick,
                                                       resist)

   4. inimitable _____   (imitate)

   5. descendant _____   (ancestor)

   6. persistent _____   (rent)

   7. insistent _____   (rent)

   8. superintendent _____   (rent)

   9. dependent _____   (rent)

   10. dependable _____   (able worker)

   11. indispensable _____   (able worker)

   12. siege _____   (city)

   13. seize _____   (neck)

   14. exhilarate _____   (hilarious)

   15. battalion _____   (battle)

III. Decide on the missing crucial letter or letters, then rewrite
the complete word.

   1. descend — nt _____   (a)

   2. depend — nt _____   (e)

   3. depend — ble _____   (a)

4. indispens — ble _____ (a)

5. s — ge _____ (ie)

6. s — ze _____ (ei)

7. vi — ify _____ (l)

8. ba — a — ion _____ (tt,l)

9. exhi — rate _____ (la)

10. irrit — ble _____ (a)

11. irr — sist — ble _____ (e,i)

12. inimit — ble _____ (a)

13. persist — nt _____ (e)

14. insist — nt _____ (e)

15. superintend — nt _____ (e)

27

How to Decide Between -*ary* and -*ery*

PROBLEMS

secret**ery** *or* secret**ary**?
monas**tery** *or* monas**tary**?
millin**ery** *or* millin**ary**?

SOLUTION

There are, in all the language, only seven important words that end in -*ery* which might tempt the unsophisticated speller into an -*ary* ending.

(A word like *very*, for extreme example, would not be in this list — no one ever has an urge to spell it *vary*. Nor would anyone be at all likely to write *brewary*, *bribary*, *finary*, *thievary*, *bakary*, *flattary*, etc., for the very obviously correct *brewery*, *bribery*, *finery*, *thievery*, *bakery*, *flattery*, etc.)

There are, on the other hand, scores and scores of words which correctly end in -*ary* which nevertheless might tempt an unsuspecting citizen into an -*ery* ending.

This fortunate circumstance makes our problem pleasantly simple. You have only to become thoroughly familiar with the seven important -*ery* words —

And then, without further thought, you can spell any other similar *doubt-producing* word with an -*ary* ending.

As it happens, the problem is even simpler than that. Let us look at four of the seven:

distill**ery** _____ millin**ery** _____

station**ery** _____ confection**ery** _____

If you drop the *y* from each of these four, you will be left with common, everyday words describing the performers of an action:

1. distill**er,** one who distills
2. station**er,** one who sells paper, etc.
3. millin**er,** one who makes hats
4. confection**er,** one who makes candies, etc.

In these instances, at least, it is hard to go wrong once you realize that *distillery, stationery, millinery,* and *confectionery* are formed by the simple addition of the letter *y* to the common, shorter forms. The obviously correct *-ery* ending is now too conspicuous to cause any further doubt.

There are three other words, however, with which you will want to develop a strong visual familiarity, words which are not formed by the simple addition of the letter *y* to shorter forms. These three are:

cemet**ery** _____ dysent**ery** _____

monast**ery** _____

And that's all there is to it. Realize that only seven words that end in *-ery* can cause any confusion. Become visually accustomed to the *-ery* ending on each of the seven. And then dismiss the problem from your mind. Every other *doubtful* word probably ends in *-ary.*

Here, for further practice, is another chance for visual and kin-esthetic review of the crucial seven:

distill**ery** _____ cemet**ery** _____

station**ery**[1] _____ monast**ery** _____

millin**ery** _____ dysent**ery** _____

confection**ery** _____

There is, then, a very simple basic principle that will effectively solve the problem of this chapter:

Point 35

There are no more than seven *doubtful* words which require *-ery* as terminal letters — in any others, if doubt exists, use *-ary.*

[1]We know from previous work with mnemonics that stationery consists of paper, etc., that stationary means standing still. See Mnemonics — Six.

TEST YOURSELF

Decide, in the following words, whether -ery or -ary is the required ending, then rewrite the complete word.

1. diction — _____ (diction**ary**)

2. station — _____ (station**ery**)
   (paper, etc.)

3. secret — _____ (secret**ary**)

4. confection — _____ (confection**ery**)

5. dignit — _____ (dignit**ary**)

6. cemet — _____ (cemet**ery**)

7. sedent — _____ (sedent**ary**)

8. distill — _____ (distill**ery**)

9. statu — _____ (statu**ary**)

10. monast — _____ (monast**ery**)

11. discretion — _____ (discretion**ary**)

12. dysent — _____ (dysent**ery**)

13. comment — _____ (comment**ary**)

14. millin — _____ (millin**ery**)

15. advers — _____ (advers**ary**)

16. station — _____ (station**ary**)
    (motionless)

(Eighteenth Day, continued)

PRETEST
1. whisky *or* whiskey?
2. tyranny *or* tyrrany?
3. definately *or* definitely?
4. proffesor *or* professor?
5. drunkeness, drunkedness *or* drunkness?

MNEMONICS
1. (whisky *or* whiskey?)

Which is correct — *whisky* or *whiskey?*

In a sense, both are correct — and you may, if you wish to insist on your rights, use whichever form appeals to you.

However, by a common custom in the liquor trade, the shorter spelling is used for one type, the longer spelling for another type.

Obviously, the type of liquor that would be most frugal in the number of letters in its name is Scotch — for which the traditional spelling is WHISK**Y** — plural: WHISK**IES**. (Canadian liquor is also spelled WHISK**Y**.) On the other hand, any American brand is WHISK**EY** — plural; WHISK**EYS**.

You may check this distinction next time you have access to a bottle of Scotch, rye, bourbon, etc.

But I suggest you make the check *before* you sample the contents — afterward you won't really care.

Correct Spellings: Scotch or

                Canadian whisk**y** _____

                domestic whisk**ey** _____

Mnemonic: Scotch is the more frugal spelling.

2. (tyranny *or* tyrrany?)

TYRANT is practically never misspelled — one is rarely tempted to use more than one *r* in this common word.

Yet the related forms TYRANNY, TYRANNOUS, and TYRANNICAL cause confusion among the most sophisticated of spellers.

The simple and effective mnemonic for all three difficult forms is the phrase "DOWN WITH TYRANTS!" This phrase, when viewed as a unit, contains two *n*'s (one in DOWN, one more in TYRANTS), and one *r* — the correct combination in each of these three confusing words.

Correct Spellings: tyranny _____

                      tyrannous _____

                      tyrannical _____

Mnemonic: "Down with tyrants!"

3. (definately *or* definitely?)

In this word, the crucial letter is the vowel after the *n*. Link DEFINITELY with the associated form DEFINITION or FINITE.

Correct Spelling: definitely _____

Mnemonics: definition, finite

4. (proffesor *or* professor?)

What, in a sense, does a PROFESSOR do? His job, you might say, is to PROFESS — and the pronunciation of the verb PROFESS is such that no combination other than one *f* and two *s*'s makes sense. Link PROFESSOR to PROFESS and you can avoid confusion as to which consonant requires doubling.

Correct Spelling: professor _____

Mnemonic: profess

5. (drunkeness, drunkedness, *or* drunkness?)

This word is one of the ten most frequently misspelled — and no wonder. The first part is simple enough — DRUNK, obviously. Just as obviously, the ending is -NESS. But what, if anything, happens in between?

Well, from educated adults to whom I propound this question I receive, generally, one of the following answers:

> *drunkness   drunkeness*
> *drunkardness   drunkedness*

None of these, unfortunately, is the correct pattern — and all of them are popular, *drunkeness* being the most prevalent misspelling. The word is properly spelled by analogy with *suddenness* (*sudden* plus -*ness*), *barrenness* (*barren* plus -*ness*), *commonness* (*common* plus -*ness*), etc. The only correct pattern, then, is DRUNK**ENN**ESS (*drunken* plus -*ness*) — all the others, logical and sound though they may seem, are totally incorrect and unacceptable.

Correct Spelling: drunk**enn**ess _____

Mnemonic: drunk**en** plus -**ness**

(All the patterns offered in the pretest were incorrect.)

TEST YOURSELF

I. Check the correct pattern.

1. Scotch (a) whisky, (b) whiskey	(a)
2. (a) tyranny, (b) tyrrany	(a)
3. (a) professor, (b) proffesor	(a)
4. (a) definately, (b) definitely	(b)
5. (a) drunkenness, (b) drunkeness	(a)

II. Recall the mnemonic for each word. (Complete Review.)

1. occu**rr**ence _____ (cu**rr**ent event)

2. superintend**ent** _____ (**rent**)

3. in**o**culate _____ (inj**e**ct)

4. indispens**able** _____ (**able** worker)

5. depend**able** _____ (**able** worker)

6. s**ie**ge _____ (c**i**ty)

7. s**ei**ze _____ (n**e**ck)

8. ba**tt**alion _____ (ba**tt**le)

9. par**all**el _____ (**all** tracks)

10. fri**ca**ss**ee** _____ (**ca**ss**e**role)

11. persist**ent** _____ (**r**ent)

12. insist**ent** _____ (**r**ent)

13. depend**ent** _____ (**r**ent)

14. emba**rr**assed _____ (**two r**obbers, Sing Sing, **ass**)

15. **an**oint _____ (**an o**il)

16. exhil**a**rate _____ (hilarious)

17. v**i**cious _____ (v**i**ce)

18. r**i**diculous _____ (r**i**dicule)

19. d**e**scription _____ (d**e**scribe)

20. rep**e**tition _____ (rep**e**at)

21. re**c**o**mm**end _____ (**c**o**mm**end)

22. b**usi**ness _____ (b**usy**)

23. ab**s**ence _____ (ab**s**ent)

24. ho**l**iday _____ (ho**l**y)

25. d**e**spair _____ (d**e**sperate)

26. **all** right _____ (**all** wrong)

27. ba**ll**oon _____ (ba**ll**)

28. p**ur**suit _____ (p**ur**se)

29. sher**iff** _____ (r**iff r**a**ff**)

30. cat**e**gory _____ (section)

31. occa**s**ional _____ (mea**s**ure)

32. va**c**uum _____ (va**c**ant)

33. station**a**ry _____ (st**a**nd)

34. station**e**ry _____ (pap**er**)

35. princip**a**l _____ (m**a**in)

36. princip**le** _____ (ru**le**)

37. separate _____ (ap**a**rt)

38. acce**l**erate _____ (ce**l**erity)

39. d**e**vise _____ (d**e**vious)

40. ir**i**descent _____ (**i**r**i**s)

41. tran**quill**ity _____ (**quill**)

42. gram**mar** _____ (**mar**)

43. pro**nun**ciation _____ (pro-**NUN**-ci-a-tion)

44. sacri**le**gious _____ (sac-**ri**-**LE**-gious)

45. gene**a**logy _____ (ge-ne-**AL**-o-gy)

46. miner**a**logy _____ (min-er-**AL**-o-gy)

47. main**ten**ance _____ (MAIN-**ten**-ance)

48. descend**ant** _____ (anc**o**stor)

49. inimitable _____ (imit**a**te)

50. irrit**a**ble _____ (irrit**a**te)

51. irresist**i**ble _____ (l**i**pstick)

52. vil**i**fy _____ (vil**e**)

53. whis**k**y _____ (Scotch)

54. whis**key** _____ (domestic)

55. tyra**nn**y, _____ ("Dow**n** with
  etc.   Tyra**n**ts!")

56. profe**ss**or _____ (to profe**ss**)

57. drunke**nn**ess _____ (drunke**n** + -**ness**)

58. defin**i**tely _____ (defin**i**tion;
                                                           fin**i**te)

III. Decide on the crucial missing letter or letters, then rewrite the complete word. (Complete Review.)

1. occu — nce _____ (rre)

2. superintend — nt _____ (e)

3. i — o — ulate _____ (n,c)

4. indispens — ble _____ (a)

5. depend — ble _____ (a)

6. s — ge _____ (ie)

7. s — ze _____ (ei)

8. ba — a — ion _____ (tt,l)

9. para — e — _____ (ll,l)

10. fri — a — ee _____ (c,ss)

11. persist — nt _____ (e)

12. insist — nt _____ (e)

13. depend — nt _____ (e)

14. emba — a — ed _____ (rr,ss)

15. a — oint _____ (n)

16. exhi — rate _____ (la)

17. vi — ious _____ (c)

18. r — diculous _____ (i)

19. d — scription _____ (e)

20. rep — tition _____ (e)

21. re — o — end _____ (c,mm)

22. bu — ness _____ (si)

23. abs — nce _____ (e)

24. ho — iday _____ (l)

25. d — spair _____ (e)

26. a — right _____ (ll)

27. ba — oon _____ (ll)

28. p — rsuit _____ (u)

29. sher — _____ (iff)

30. cat — gory _____ (e)

31. occa — ional _____ (s)

32. va — uum _____ (c)

33. station — ry _____ (a)
    (fixed)

34. station — ry _____ (e)
    (paper)

35. princip — _____ (al)
    (main)

36. princip — _____ (le)
    (rúle)

37. sep — rate _____ (a)

38. acce — erate _____ (l)

39. d — vise _____ (e)

40. i — idescent _____ (r)

41. tranqui — ity _____ (ll)

42. gramm — r _____ (a)

43. pron — nciation _____ (u)

44. sacr — l — gious _____ (i,e)

45. gene — logy _____ (a)

46. miner — logy _____ (a)

47. maint — nance _____ (e)

48. descend — nt _____ (a)

49. inimit — ble _____ (a)

50. irrit — ble _____ (a)

51. irresist — ble _____ (i)

52. vi — ify _____ (l)

53. whisk — (Scotch) _____ (y)

54. whisk — (others) _____   (ey)

55. ty — a — y _____   (r,nn)

56. pro — e — or _____   (f,ss)

57. drunk — ess _____   (enn)

58. defin — ly _____   (ite)

28

How to Make an Accurate Decision
Between -*able* and -*ible*

PROBLEM
    detest**able** *or* detest**ible**?
    irrit**able** *or* irrit**ible**?
    abomin**able** *or* abomin**ible**?
    predict**able** *or* predict**ible**?

SOLUTION
    A word may correctly end in -*able*, say *detestable* or *presentable*.
    Another word may correctly end in -*ible*, say *digestible* or *corruptible*.
    The last syllables of all four words are identical in pronunciation
— yet for two of them we write -*able*, for the other two -*ible*.
    Why?
    The final answer often lies in the Latin derivation of the word,
as it does in -*ence* -*ance* forms — but it would then seem that only
a scholar of the classics would be able unerringly to make an
accurate and self-assured choice.
    Which would be unfortunate — for there are so many hundreds of
words that end in either -*able* or -*ible*, most of them common enough
to be used over and over again in everyday writing, that only the
Latin students could be expected to write an error-free paper.
    Fortunately there is a fact which weighs heavily in favor of your
learning to feel completely in control of the -*able* -*ible* problem even
if you have never studied Latin.
    This fact is:

With no more than a normal number of exceptions, all -able and -ible words fall into easily learned and sharply differentiated groups.

To the uninitiated, the problem of whether to end a word with -*able* or -*ible* is a source of never-ending confusion —

To the sophisticated speller who is familiar with basic principles of English spelling patterns, it is no problem at all.

And it need be no problem to you —

If you become thoroughly familiar with every relevant characteristic of each of the -*able* and -*ible* groups —

And if, in addition —

You make a complete intellectual, visual, and kinesthetic adjustment to the typical examples that will be offered in each group.

As a result of such training, you will eventually be able to put all doubts and hesitation out of your mind when you have to decide between ending a word with -*able* or -*ible*.

A big promise? Yes, but in this instance easy to fulfill.

If we thread our way cautiously and patiently through the applicable principles, as we usually do, a seemingly complicated and troublesome problem can be mastered with almost no pain.

Follow me carefully, now, step by step.

We shall consider in this chapter six groups of -*able* words.

Group I. The Root Is a Full Word

Notice these typical examples:

detest**able** _____   perish**able** _____

predict**able** _____   person**able** _____

avail**able** _____   correct**able** _____

depend**able** _____   detect**able** _____

You will observe, in each case, that if you drop the -*able* ending you have left a full, acceptable, everyday word:

detest	avail	perish	correct
predict	depend	person	detect

Which permits us to formulate a basic principle:

Point 36

Roots usually end in -*able* if, in their own right, they are full, acceptable English words.

Here are some more examples out of hundreds. Drop the *-able* in each case and a full word is left.

mail**able** _____	present**able** _____
profit**able** _____	credit**able** _____
accept**able** _____	break**able** _____
	etc.

Group II. *The Root is a Full Word Lacking Final* e
Now examine these typical examples:

blam**able** _____	debat**able** _____
deplor**able** _____	excit**able** _____
desir**able** _____	presum**able** _____

You will observe here a new common factor — if you drop *-able* you have left a root lacking only a final *-e* to be a full word:

$$blam(e) \quad desir(e) \quad excit(e)$$
$$deplor(e) \quad debat(e) \quad presum(e)$$

Which permits us to formulate our second principle:

Point 37
Forms usually are spelled with an *-able* ending if the root needs only a final *-e* to be a full word.

Here are more and similar examples to illustrate Point 37: Note, in each case, that if *-able* is dropped a full word lacking only final *-e* remains.

lovable _____	valu**able** _____
pleasur**able** _____	us**able** _____
siz**able** _____	(in)describ**able** _____

Group III. *The Root Ends in* i
Examine these words, looking again for a common element:

appreci**able** _____	reli**able** _____
envi**able** _____	satisfi**able** _____
justifi**able** _____	soci**able** _____

Impossible to escape is the common letter *i* preceding each ending. Obviously *-able* is the only sane suffix, else we would have a double *i*, a scarce and un-American combination. So we now have a third basic principle:

Point 38
-able is always found after the letter *i.*

Group IV. *The Root Has Other Forms Built on the Letter* -a
Consider these typical examples:

demonstr**able** _____   inflamm**able** _____

du**rable** _____   inviol**able** _____

repar**able** _____   inflamm**able** _____

Here the common element may be somewhat less easy to detect. When we drop *-able,* we do not have a full word left, with or without an added *e* — but suppose we think of other forms of these words:

    (demonstr**able**) demonstrate   (irrit**able**) irritate
    (du**rable**) duration   (inviol**able**) violate
    (repar**able**) reparations   (inflamm**able**) inflammation

And there it is, the common element we've been looking for — each root can be formed into a word containing as a principal vowel the letter *a* — hence the ending *-able.* So we can now understand a fourth basic principle:

Point 39
A root will generally require an *-able* ending if there are other forms of the word which contain *a* as the principal vowel.
Take some more examples to illustrate Point 39.

(pregnant) impregn**able** _____   (estimate) estim**able** _____

(delectation) delect**able** _____   (imitate) inimit**able** _____

(hospitality) hospit**able** _____   (tolerate) intoler**able** _____

(penetrate) impenetr**able** _____   (separate) insepar**able** _____

(abomination) abomin**able** _____   (enumerate) innumer**able** _____

Group V.   The Root Ends in Hard c *or* g

Notice, in the following forms, the letter preceding *-able*, and pay particular attention to how that letter is pronounced:

despic**able** _____   applic**able** _____

educ**able** _____   amic**able** _____

implac**able** _____   practic**able** _____

explic**able** _____   navig**able** _____

revoc**able** _____   indefatig**able** _____

The letter preceding the *-able* ending is in each instance either c or *g;* moreover, both letters have hard pronunciations — c as in *cat,* g as in *go.*

Now this is no surprise.

We know from earlier chapters that *a* is a hardening vowel — if c or g is hard in pronunciation, only *-able* will retain this hardness; *-ible* (since the letter *i* is a softening vowel) will soften a letter which we wish to keep hard.

So we can easily formulate a fifth principle:

Point 40

-able is the only possible ending after a hard c or g, in order to maintain the required pronunciation.

These five groupings have taken care of whatever uniformities exist in *-able* patterns —

They give you a good, fast, running start on making an accurate decision as to whether to end a word with *-able* or *-ible.*

For you know that *-able* is probably[1] the required ending under *any one* of the following circumstances:

1. If the root is a full word in its own right (*govern*-able, *impression*-able, *respect*-able, etc.)

2. If the root is a full word lacking only the final *e* (*blam*-able, *believ*-able, *palat*-able, etc.)

3. If the preceding letter is *i*, in order to avoid a double *i* combination (*soci*-able, *justifi*-able, *certifi*-able, etc.)

---

[1] I say "probably" because of course there will be exceptions to some of these principles. These we shall consider in due time.

4. If the root has another form built on *a* as the principal vowel (irritable — irritate, demonstrable — demonstrate, etc.)

5. If the preceding letter is a c or *g* that is pronounced hard (applicable, navigable, etc.)

These five points alone can give you self-assured command over several hundred *-able* words — only a few of the available examples were used to illustrate each principle.

Group VI. Exceptional Cases

There are a number of important words ending in *-able* which do not fit into any of the five groups discussed. These you have no choice but to become familiar with *visually,* so that only *-able* looks proper and *-ible* seems unfamiliar, unpleasant, and therefore incorrect.

I'll list the words — commit each one as firmly as you can to visual memory, writing each form in the blank provided.

1. equitable _____

2. formidable _____

3. inexorable _____

4. inevitable _____

5. memorable _____

6. probable _____

7. unconscionable _____

8. portable _____

9. arable _____

10. ineffable _____

11. potable _____

12. inscrutable _____

13. insuperable _____

14. indomitable _____

15. malleable _____

16. vulnerable _____

17. affable _____

18. palpable _____

19. culpable _____

(These nineteen words fit into no particular category — they must be learned individually.)

29

How to Recognize a Root That Requires
an -*ible* Suffix

PROBLEMS
collaps**able** *or* collaps**ible**?
contempt**able** *or* contempt**ible**?
resist**able** *or* resist**ible**?
connect**able** *or* connect**ible**?

SOLUTION
You know that if a root is a full word, or a full word except for the final *e*, the likely ending will be -*able*.

You know, also, that -*able* attaches to three types of roots that are not full words:

1. Those that end in the letter *i* —

(*insati*-**able**, etc.)

2. Those that have other forms built on *a* as the principal vowel —

(inimit**able** — imit**a**te, etc.)

3. Those that end in *hard c* or *g* —

(irrevo**cable**, indefati**gable**, etc.)

And you know, also, that there are nineteen special -*able* roots which are not full words and do not fit into any of the three categories listed above.

All right — that should be clear enough by now.

And there should be an equally clear implication that -*ible* is the proper ending for roots which are *not* full words (or full words

217

lacking final e), and which do not end in the letter *i* or in hard c or
g, and which furthermore do not belong among the nineteen special
cases considered in the previous chapter.

Note, then, how the following *-ible* forms are built on "non-word"
roots which do not fit into any previously established *-able* categories. (The root is italicized so that you can see at a glance that
it is not, by itself, a real word.)

Group I. *The Root Is Not a Full Word*

*aud*ible _____	*ostens*ible _____
*compat*ible _____	*poss*ible _____
*cred*ible _____	*terr*ible _____
*divis*ible _____	*horr*ible _____
*vis*ible _____	*dirig*ible _____
*feas*ible _____	*neglig*ible _____
*plaus*ible _____	*ed*ible _____
*combust*ible _____	*infall*ible _____
*suscept*ible _____	*tang*ible _____
*ris*ible _____	*intellig*ible _____
*incorrig*ible _____	*indel*ible _____
*irasc*ible _____	

These are by no means all, or even most, of the *-ible* forms which
are built on non-word roots; but there are enough to emphasize that
non-word roots *other than the -able types we have discussed* can be
presumed to require an *-ible* ending. We can, in fact, now formulate
our first basic *-ible* principle:

Point 41

Non-word roots which do not fall into previous *-able* categories
will require an *-ible* ending.

You realize now that special kinds of non-word roots take *-able*,
that otherwise a non-word root takes *-ible*.

The next question that may occur to you is, do all *full-word* roots require *-able?*

The answer, unfortunately, is no.

There is a special type of full-word root which ends in *-ible.*

Namely, that root which forms a noun by the *immediate* addition of the suffix *-ion.*

For example:

(collect — collec*tion*) collect**ible** _____

(digest — diges*tion*) digest**ible** _____

(corrupt — corrup*tion*) corrupt**ible** _____

(exhaust — exhaus*tion*) inexhaust**ible** _____

Notice that I say "by the *immediate* addition of the suffix *-ion.*"

So that roots like *expect, excite, detest, present,* etc., would not fit into this category. Notice that such roots add *-ation,* not an immediate *ion:*

(expect — expect*ation*) expect**able** _____

(detest — detest*ation*) detest**able** _____

(present — present*ation*) present**able** _____

(excite — excit*ation*) excit**able** _____

Now examine the type of root which adds an immediate *-ion* suffix:

Group II. The Root Is a Full Word That Has an Immediate -ion *Form*

(collect — collec*tion*) collect**ible** _____

(digest — diges*tion*) digest**ible** _____

(corrupt — corrup*tion*) corrupt**ible** _____

(exhaust — exhaus*tion*) (in)exhaust**ible** _____

(affect — affec*tion*) affect**ible** _____

(contract — contrac*tion*) contract**ible** _____

(connect — connec*tion*) connect**ible** _____

(convert — conver*sion*[1]) convert**ible** _____

(access — acces**sion**) acces**sible** _____

(corrode — corro*sion*[2]) corrod**ible** _____

(expanse — expan*sion*) expan**sible** _____

(perfect — perfec*tion*) perfect**ible** _____

(reverse — rever*sion*) revers**ible**   _____

(suggest — sugges*tion*) suggest**ible** _____

But how about *predict, detect,* and *correct?*
These words have immediate *-ion* forms: *prediction, detection, correction.*
And yet they have *-able* endings!
Namely:

predict**able** _____   correct**able** _____

detect**able** _____

So these three have to be considered special exceptions, and we would formulate our basic principle as follows:

Point 42
With the exception of *predictable, detectable,* and *correctable,* a full-word root that can add an immediate *-ion* is likely to have an *-ible* ending.

You know so far that *non-word roots,* other than special types, take an *-ible* ending.
And you know that *full-word roots* that have immediate *-ion* forms also take an *-ible* ending (excepting *predictable, correctable,* and *detectable*).
Let us now examine a third type of *-ible* word.

Group III. The Root Ends in -ns *or* -miss

defen**sible** _____   reprehen**sible** _____

indefen**sible** _____   sen**sible** _____

[1] *t* changes to *s*, which does not alter the principle.
[2] *d* changes to *s*, which again does not affect the principle.

comprehen**sible** _____   insen**sible** _____

incomprehen**sible** _____   expan**sible** _____

respon**sible** _____   transm**issible** _____

irrespon**sible** _____   adm**issible** _____

osten**sible** _____   perm**issible** _____

disten**sible** _____   dism**issible** _____

This is simple enough. While some of these words would also fit into Groups I or II (the root of *comprehensible* is not a full word; the root of *admissible* has an immediate *-ion* ending — *admission*, etc.), still an *-ns* or *-miss* root immediately alerts you to end your word in *-ible* rather than *-able*.

Except, of course, for our old friend INDISPENS**ABLE**!

You see, now, why the temptation is so great to use an *-ible* ending on this word — practically every other *-ns* form requires it.

But *indispensable* links up with *dependable* and is a word over which the mnemonic **"ABLE** worker" has given you full control.

So we are ready for our third basic principle:

Point 43

If the root ends in *-ns* or *-miss*, use *-ible*, except in *indispensable* (or, of course, *dispensable*).

Our next type of *-ible* words may also fit into previous categories, but will contain so conspicuous a common factor that we shall examine it in a separate group.

Group IV.   The Root Ends in Soft c *or* g

invin**cible** _____   convin**cible** _____

for**cible** _____   redu**cible** _____

coer**cible** _____   irredu**cible** _____

sedu**cible** _____   produ**cible** _____

indu**cible** _____   incorri**gible** _____

dedu**cible** _____   intan**gible** _____

negli**gible** _____   intelli**gible** _____

eli**gible** _____   le**gible** _____

ille**gible** _____

In each of these instances the c is pronounced soft — like an *s;* or the *g* is pronounced soft — like a *j.* If *-able* were the suffix, c and *g* would be hard — clearly only *-ible* is possible.

These words will of course remind you of those demons with soft c and *g* which we discussed in Chapters 12 and 14. There the correct ending was *-able* and the e had to be retained to keep c or *g* soft. You will recall:

enfor**ceable** _____   char**geable** _____

embra**ceable** _____   brid**geable** _____

la**ceable** _____   chan**geable** _____

repla**ceable** _____   mana**geable** _____

irrepla**ceable** _____   dispara**geable** _____

pronoun**ceable** _____   enga**geable** _____

tra**ceable** _____   discoura**geable** _____

servi**ceable** _____   marria**geable** _____

boun**ceable** _____   enra**geable** _____

pea**ceable** _____   salva**geable** _____

noti**ceable** _____   mortga**geable** _____

jud**geable** _____

This need not be at all confusing. You have already made a strong adjustment to the *-ceable* and *-geable* words of Chapters 12 and 14, and these new *-cible* and *-gible* words can be easily separated in your mind from the previous groups you have studied.

To begin with, notice that every *-ceable* and *-geable* root is a word in its own right if final *-e* is retained: *enforce, embrace, notice, charge, change, marriage,* etc.

But of the *-cible* and *-gible* roots only the *duc-* forms plus three others (*coerce—coercible, force—forcible, convince—convincible*) are full words if final *-e* is retained.

Keeping these factors in mind, let us formulate our next basic principle:

Point 44

Roots ending in soft *-c* or soft *-g* require the *-ible* ending. These roots are usually not full words, with the exception of *coercible, forcible, convincible,* and the *-ducible* group.

Group V. Exceptional Cases

We are ready, now, for the comparatively few instances of *-ible* words which do not fit into one of the four previous groups. Like the nineteen special *-able* words, these too must be mastered by visual and kinesthetic memory.

1. contempt**ible** _____   5. inflex**ible** _____

2. gull**ible** _____   6. resist**ible** _____

3. collaps**ible** _____   7. irresist**ible** _____

4. flex**ible** _____   8. discern**ible** _____

Eight forms, all of them full words when the ending is dropped (contempt-**ible**, gull-**ible**, discern-**ible**, resist-**ible**, etc.). And no root has an *-ion* form. So they should all be *-able* forms — that they are not makes them exceptional cases.

Let us now chart, for quick and successful review, all we know about *-able* and *-ible* words.

COMPLETE LAYOUT ON *-able* AND *-ible* WORDS

THE *-ABLE* ENDING IS ATTACHED TO:	THE *-IBLE* ENDING IS ATTACHED TO:
1. Roots that are full words in their own right — *surmount*-able, etc.	1. Roots that are not full words in their own right — *vis*-ible, etc. *EXCEPT* special "non-word" *-able* forms
2. Roots that are full words lacking only final *e.* — *ador(e)*-able, etc.	2. Roots that are full words in their own right and which have immediate *-ion* forms. — *express-ion*—inexpressible, etc. *EXCEPT* predictable, detectable, and correctable.

COMPLETE LAYOUT ON -*able* AND -*ible* WORDS (*continued*)

THE -*ABLE* ENDING IS ATTACHED TO:	THE -*IBLE* ENDING IS ATTACHED TO:
3. Roots ending in the letter -*i*. — *ami*-able, etc.	3. Roots that end in -*ns* or -*miss* — defe*ns*-ible, ad*miss*-ible, etc. *EXCEPT dispensable* and *indispensable*.
4. Roots that have other forms built on -*a* as the principal vowel. — cap*a*ble — cap*a*city, etc.	4. No similar category.
5. Roots that end in *hard* -*c* or -*g* — communicable, navigable, etc.	5. Roots that end in *soft* -*c* or -*g* — seducible, negligible, etc. These roots are usually not full words, with the exception of *coercible*[1], *forcible*[1], *convincible*[1], and the -*ducible* group.
6. Roots that keep the softening -*e* after -*c* or -*g* — noticeable, manageable, etc.	6. No similar category.

And recall the nineteen exceptional cases under -*able*, the eight exceptional cases under -*ible*. Let us review these once again:

-*ABLE FORMS*

1. equit**able** _____

2. formid**able** _____

3. inexor**able** _____

4. inevit**able** _____

5. memor**able** _____

6. prob**able** _____

7. unconscion**able** _____

8. port**able** _____

9. ar**able** _____

10. ineff**able** _____

11. pot**able** _____

12. inscrut**able** _____

[1]When final -*e* is replaced, we have *coerce, force, convince*, etc.

13. insuper**able** _____   17. aff**able** _____

14. indomit**able** _____   18. palp**able** _____

15. malle**able** _____   19. culp**able** _____

16. vulner**able** _____

-IBLE FORMS

1. contempt**ible** _____   5. collaps**ible** _____

2. gull**ible** _____   6. discern**ible** _____

3. flex**ible** _____   7. resist**ible** _____

4. inflex**ible** _____   8. irresist**ible** _____

TEST YOURSELF

Add the correct ending (*-able* or *-ible*) to the following roots, re-writing the complete word.

I. *Full Words*

1. depend — _____ (able)

2. companion — _____ (able)

3. detest — _____ (ablc)

4. predict — _____ (able)

5. detect — _____ (able)

6. correct — _____ (able)

7. present — _____ (able)

8. remark — _____ (able)

9. miser — _____ (able)

10. pass — _____ (able)

II. *Root a Full Word Lacking -e*

11. excit — _____ (able)

12. lov — _____ (able)

13. argu — _____ (able)

14. excus — _____ (able)

15. mov — _____ (able)

16. desir — _____ (able)

17. valu — _____ (able)

18. ador — _____ (able)

19. deplor — _____ (able)

20. debat — _____ (able)

III. Root Ends in -i

21. ami — _____ (able)

22. soci — _____ (able)

23. classifi — _____ (able)

24. envi — _____ (able)

IV. Root Has Other Forms Built on the Letter -a

25. commend — (commendation) _____ (able)

26. irrit — (irritation) _____ (able)

27. cap — (capacity) _____ (able)

28. (in)separ — (separate) _____ (able)

29. (in)toler — (tolerate) _____ (able)

V. Root ends in Hard -c or -g

30. applic — _____ (able)

31. explic — _____ (able)

32. navig — _____ (able)

33. indefatig — _____ (able)

34. revoc — _____ (able)

35. implac — _____ (able)

VI. Root is a "Non-Word"

36. aud — _____ (ible)

37. plaus — _____ (ible)

38. feas — _____ (ible)

39. ris — _____ (ible)

40. horr — _____ (ible)

41. combust — _____ (ible)

VII. Root Has an -ion Form

42. collect — (collection) _____ (ible)

43. indestruct — (destruction) _____ (ible)

44. convert — (conversion) _____ (ible)

45. incorrupt — (corruption) _____ (ible)

VIII. Root Ends in Soft -c or -g

46. evinc — _____ (ible)

47. forc — _____ (ible)

48. neglig — _____ (ible)

49. intellig — _____ (ible)

50. elig — _____ (ible)

51. irreduc — _____ (ible)

52. illeg — _____ (ible)

53. intang — _____ (ible)

54. incorrig — _____ (ible)

IX. Root Ends in Soft -c or -g and Retains the -e

55. enforce — _____ (able)

56. notice — _____ (able)

57. manage — _____ (able)

58. change — _____ (able)

59. marriage — _____ (able)

X. Exceptional Cases

60. port — _____ (able)

61. inevit — _____ (able)

62. formid — _____ (able)

63. insuper — _____ (able)

64. vulner — _____ (able)

65. aff — _____ (able)

66. culp — _____ (able)

67. contempt — _____ (ible)

68. flex — _____ (ible)

69. collaps — _____ (ible)

70. (ir)resist — _____ (ible)

71. discern — _____ (ible)

XI. Root Ends in -ns or -miss

72. (in)defens — _____ (ible)

73. reprehens — _____ (ible)

74. (ir)respons — _____ (ible)

75. (in)sens — _____ (ible)

76. (in)comprehens — _____ (ible)

77. admiss — _____ (ible)

78. permiss — _____ (ible)

79. transmiss — _____ (ible)

80. (in)dispens — _____ (able)

81. ostens — _____ (ible)

How to Decide Between -er and -or

PROBLEM
commentater *or* commentator?
elevater *or* elevator?
visiter *or* visitor?
better *or* bettor?

SOLUTION
The *-or -er* problem is not so common that we need make a big thing out of it. Both suffixes mean either "one who" or "that which" (*investor*, one who *invests; elevator*, that which *raises*), and there is no uniformity governing the use of the proper ending. *-Er* is the sensible form, since it follows the pronunciation — but far more words end in *-or* than in *-er*. Most educated people have developed an unconscious visual reaction to *-er -or* words, and have trouble only with a few isolated forms.

And their trouble always takes this shape: they are tempted to write *-er* when *-or* is correct, rarely the other way around.

So a good, serviceable, trustworthy principle can be formulated:

POINT 45
When in doubt, use *-or* rather than *-er* as an ending with the meaning of "one who" or "that which."

Let me present twenty of the occasionally troublesome forms. Develop a keen visual reaction to them, practice each one kinesthetically, and the chances are very good that this problem, if it is present at all, will vanish.

Occasionally Misspelled Words Ending in -or

1. aviator _____	11. radiator _____
2. educator _____	12. supervisor _____
3. distributor _____	13. survivor _____
4. elevator _____	14. visitor _____
5. escalator _____	15. prevaricator _____
6. impostor _____	16. fabricator _____
7. indicator _____	17. accelerator _____
8. investigator _____	18. protector _____
9. commentator _____	19. spectator _____
10. predecessor _____	20. administrator _____

And of course there is also *bettor,* one who makes a *bet,* not to be confused with *better,* the comparative of *good.*

TEST YOURSELF

Add the proper ending (*-or* or *-er*) to each root; then rewrite the complete word.

1. surviv — _____ (or)

2. administrat — _____ (or)

3. spectat — _____ (or)

4. protect — _____ (or)

5. accelerat — _____ (or)

6. fabricat — _____ (or)

7. prevaricat — _____ (or)

8. visit — _____ (or)

9. supervis — _____ (or)

10. radiat — _____ (or)

11. predecess — _____ (or)

12. commentat — _____ (or)

13. investigat — _____ (or)

14. indicat — _____ (or)

15. impost — _____ (or)

16. escalat — _____ (or)

17. elevat — _____ (or)

18. distribut — _____ (or)

19. educat — _____ (or)

20. aviat — _____ (or)

31

Fourth Review

And now your training is complete

In Chapters 26–30 we have covered the basic principles that govern the remaining problems — -*ance* or -*ence*?, -*ary* or -*ery*?, -*able* or -*ible*?, and -*er* or -*or*?

As to the problem of -*ance* or -*ence*, you have learned:

1. That the special group of verbs which end in single -*r* preceded by a single vowel, *and accented on the final syllable*, all form nouns in -*ence*.

   refer**ence** _____ abhor**ence** _____
                              etc.

2. That otherwise only visual and kinesthetic practice can help you make a correct choice.

3. And that, if you are still in serious doubt, -*ence* is the likely ending, owing to its greater numerical occurrence.

As to the problem of -*ary* or -*ery*, you have learned:

4. That -*ary* is by far the commoner ending.

5. But that -*ery* is correct in seven important words, namely:

   1. distill**ery** _____   4. confection**ery** _____

   2. station**ery** _____   5. cemet**ery** _____
      (paper)   6. monast**ery** _____

   3. millin**ery** _____   7. dysent**ery** _____

As to the problem of -*able* or -*ible*, you have learned:

6. That *-able* attaches to most full-word roots.

   predict-**able** _____ depend-**able** _____

   etc.

7. That *-able* attaches to most full-word roots lacking only final *-e*.

   deplor(e)-**able** _____ debat(e)-**able** _____

   etc.

8. That *-able* attaches to roots ending in the letter *-i*.

   justifi-**able** _____ reli-**able** _____

   etc.

9. That *-able* attaches to roots which have other forms built on *-a* as a principal vowel.

   (imit**a**te) inimit**able** _____ (irrit**a**te) irrit**able** _____

   etc.

10. That *-able* attaches to roots ending in hard *-c* or *-g*.

    navig**able** _____ practic**able** _____

11. And that, finally, *-able* attaches to nineteen special roots which have no common characteristics. These are:

    1. equit**able** _____
    2. formid**able** _____
    3. inexor**able** _____
    4. inevit**able** _____
    5. memor**able** _____
    6. prob**able** _____
    7. unconscion**able** _____
    8. port**able** _____
    9. ar**able** _____
    10. ineff**able** _____
    11. pot**able** _____
    12. inscrut**able** _____
    13. insuper**able** _____
    14. indomit**able** _____
    15. malle**able** _____
    16. vulner**able** _____
    17. aff**able** _____
    18. palp**able** _____
    19. culp**able** _____

12. That, on the other hand, *-ible* attaches to most *non-word* roots.

audible _____ divisible _____
etc.

13. That *-ible* attaches to full-word roots that have an immediate *-ion* form.

digestible _____ corruptible _____
etc.

14. That the exceptions to Statement 13 are:

predictable _____ correctable _____

detectable _____

15. That *-ible* attaches to roots ending in *-ns* or *-miss*.

comprehensible _____ admissible _____
etc.

16. That the important exceptions to Statement 15 are:

dispensable _____ indispensable _____

17. That *-ible* attaches to roots ending in soft *-g* or soft *-c*.

invincible _____ intangible _____
etc.

18. That Statement 17 excludes the special *-able* words in which a softening *-e* is retained after *-g* or *-c*.

serviceable _____ manageable _____
etc.

19. And that, finally, *-ible* attaches to eight special roots which have no common characteristics. These are:

contemptible _____ collapsible _____

gullible _____ resistible _____

flexible _____ irresistible _____

inflexible _____ discernible _____

As to the problem of *-er* or *-or*, you have learned:

20. That mistakes are rarely made in words that end in -er; therefore, when in doubt, you are probably safe in using the -or ending.
21. That otherwise you must rely on your kinesthetic and visual memory, as no general principle effectively separates the chaff from the wheat — or the lambs from the goats.

FOURTH REVIEW TEST

I. Decide whether -ance or -ence attaches to each root, then rewrite the complete word.

1. refer — _____ (ence)

2. resist — _____ (ance)

3. persever — _____ (ance)

4. occurr— _____ (ence)

5. transfer — _____ (ence)

6. admitt — _____ (ance)

7. deliver — _____ (ance)

8. confid — _____ (ence)

9. exist — _____ (ence)

10. mainten — _____ (ance)

11. abund — _____ (ance)

12. irrelev — _____ (ance)

II. Decide whether -ery or -ary attaches to each root, then rewrite the complete word.

1. secret — _____ (ary)

2. monast — _____ (ery)

3. millin — _____ (ery)

4. confection — _____ (ery)

5. cemet — _____ (ery)

6. dysent — _____ (ery)

7. diction — _____ (ary)

III. Decide whether *-able* or *-ible* attaches to each root, then rewrite the complete word.

(Full words)

1. detest — _____ (able)

2. depend — _____ (able)

3. accept — _____ (able)

(Full words lacking -e)

4. deplor — _____ (able)

5. excit — _____ (able)

(*i* ending)

6. envi — _____ (able)

7. soci — _____ (able)

(Other forms with -*a*)

8. irrit — _____ (able)

9. inimit — _____ (able)

10. abomin — _____ (able)

(Hard c or *g*)

11. despic — _____ (able)

12. indefatig — _____ (able)

(Non-words)

13. compat — _____ (ible)

14. feas — _____ (ible)

15. plaus — _____ (ible)

16. combust — _____ (ible)

17. infall — _____ (ible)

18. suscept — _____ (ible)

(Full words with immediate -ion forms)

19. collect — _____ (ible)

20. digest — _____ (ible)

21. corrupt — _____ (ible)

22. connect — _____ (ible)

23. perfect — _____ (ible)

24. suggest — _____ (ible)

(Exceptions to above)

25. predict — _____ (able)

26. detect — _____ (able)

27. correct — _____ (able)

(Root ends in -ns or -miss)

28. defens — _____ (ible)

29. admiss — _____ (ible)

30. incomprehens — _____ (ible)

31. permiss — _____ (ible)

(Exception to above)

32. indispens — _____ (able)

(Soft -c or -g)

33. invinc — _____ (ible)

34. forc — _____ (ible)

35. neglig — _____ (ible)

36. irreduc — _____ (ible)

(Artificially softened -c or -g)

37. enforce — _____ (able)

38. notice — _____ (able)

39. charge — _____ (able)

40. manage — _____ (able)

(Special exceptions)

41. equit — _____ (able)

42. insuper — _____ (able)

43. vulner — _____ (able)

44. formid — _____ (able)

45. culp — _____ (able)

46. contempt — _____ (ible)

47. inflex — _____ (ible)

48. collaps — _____ (ible)

49. irresist — _____ (ible)

IV. Decide whether *-er* or *-or* attaches to each root, then rewrite the complete word.

1. commentat — _____ (or)

2. elevat — _____ (or)

3. visit — _____ (or)

4. investigat — _____ (or)

5. surviv — _____ (or)

32

How to Avoid British and Other Ostentatious Spellings

PROBLEMS
   honour *or* honor?
   glamour *or* glamor?
   aesthetic *or* esthetic?
   cheque *or* check?

SOLUTION

American spelling is sufficiently illogical, contradictory, ironic, and uncontrollable without our going out of our way to make it even more so.

Of this I am sure you are now convinced, if indeed you did not have that conviction long before you picked up this book.

Efforts have been made for years to simplify our patterns and combinations, and I am sorry to have to tell you that very little progress can be reported.   Attempts to make such pronunciation-spellings as *laf* (laugh), *fotograf* (photograph), *hed* (head), *nife* (knife), *activ* (active), *dout* (doubt), and *tuf* (tough) acceptable and popular have met with the most ignominious failure, as you can appreciate — yet some forward steps have been taken and it would be only the most die-hard and obstinate reactionary who would refuse to accept those comparatively new and logical patterns which are now in widespread and preferable use.

For example, Column I shows former spellings which have almost universally given way to the modern forms in Column II.

I. Old Spellings	*II. Modern Forms*
aesthetic	esthetic
aeroplane	airplane[1]
aeon	eon
oesophagus	esophagus
encyclopaedia	encyclopedia
mediaeval	medieval
foetus	fetus
anaemia	anemia
programme	program
quartette	quartet
centre	center
metre	meter
calibre	caliber
fibre	fiber
manoeuvre	maneuver
theatre	theater
mould	mold
moult	molt

Most of these older spellings are particularly popular in England, and there are Britons who sneer at our simpler forms — the fact remains, nevertheless, that in American spelling the modern combinations are not only preferable but almost universally found in all writing of however formal a character.

(A few words, despite their illogical and old-fashioned appearance hold on tenaciously to popular fancy in America — for example, the older form *gauge* is more prevalent than the modern *gage*, and *aerial* is still the only permissible pattern.)

British spelling is in many instances different, almost startlingly so, from American patterns, and usually more complicated, and it would be unwise and conspicuous, to say the least, if not actually ostentatious, to become too thoroughly addicted to British forms.

---

[1] There are those fence-sitters who compromise by writing *airoplane* — but this bastardized pattern, I am happy to report, has no sanction whatever.

In England, for example, the *-our* ending is prevalent: *honour, labour, behaviour, demeanour, humour, flavour, neighbour,* etc. American style always drops the unnecessary *-u,* preferring *honor, labor, behavior, demeanor, humor, flavor, neighbor,* etc.

(*Glamour,* however, is the preferable American spelling, perhaps because it has a certain air about it — but the adjective is correctly written *glamorous.*)

British spelling tends to use an *-yse* or *-ise* ending where we prefer *-yze* and *-ize* — Englishmen will write *analyse, paralyse, civilise, apologise,* etc., for our *analyze, paralyze, civilize, apologize,* etc. And Britons prefer *kerb* to *curb, tyre* to *tire, gaol* to *jail, enquiry* to *inquiry, storey* to *story* (for the floors of a building), *cheque* to *check,* and *racquet* to *racket* (that is, in tennis or badminton — our *racket* as an illegal enterprise or a great noise is also the British spelling).

In England *plough* is written for *plow; defence, offence,* and *pretence* for *defense, offense,* and *pretense,* and *connexion, inflexion,* and *reflexion* for *connection, inflection,* and *reflection.* (But *complexion* is the only acceptable form on both sides of the ocean.)

There is also the British tendency to double a consonant in verb forms where we prefer to leave it alone — *cancelled, traveller, travelled, jeweller, jewelled,* etc. American preference is for the single *-l* in these and similar words — indeed American preference is always for the simpler, closer-to-pronunciation spelling.

You are always safer using the simpler, American pattern in any word — British spelling may give an interesting continental air to your writing but it will also invest it with a stiff and unfamiliar appearance.

How far can you go in simplifying your spelling? You have probably seen *thru, tho, altho, thoro, thoroly, nite,* and *thot* (*thought*) in informal communications — and for such writing these may be acceptable to a degree. In any kind of business or formal letters they are considered out of place. It is true that they may show a refreshing freedom from conventional spelling habits rather than ignorance, but when you spell correctly you give up your right to freedom and have to accept almost complete conformity to rules and custom, which is all that English spelling generally is.

Unless you agree with that notoriously poor speller, Andrew Jackson, our seventh President, who, you recall, claimed that "It is a dammed poor mind that can think of only one way to spell a word."

According to one story, which may or may not be authentic but which makes awfully good telling, President Jackson originated the phrase "O.K." When government documents came to his desk, so the story goes, he would read them through and if he found them in proper order he would scrawl O.K. at the bottom and initial them. Why O.K.? Well, it's perfectly simple — Jackson was abbreviating *all correct,* which he spelled *"orl korrect"*!

So maybe the "dammed poor mind" attitude was a thinly veiled excuse for ignorance rather than a courageous expression of healthy rebellion....

33

How to Continue Your Improvement

in Spelling

The training program you have just finished —

Has given you mastery over the important basic principles of English spelling —

Has probably eliminated most of your *unconscious* errors —

Has developed in you complete and perhaps automatic control over the kinds of words commonly and consistently misspelled by the average literate person —

Has sharpened your visual and kinesthetic memory of the correct patterns of these words to such a degree that you can now spell them not only without error but also without doubts, misgivings or hesitation —

Has eliminated the causes of any insecurity or confusion about the proper forms of troublesome demons —

Has helped you come to terms with the contradictions, complexities, paradoxes and inconsistencies of the system of spelling under which we operate —

Has made you, if you have worked carefully and conscientiously, a competent, self-assured and perhaps near-perfect speller.

This program has probably eliminated close to 98 per cent of the errors you have been in the habit of making or were likely to make.

For further improvement, if there happens to be room for such improvement, you need to discover the special, uncommon, it may be *unconscious*, errors not covered by your training.

It is possible that a small number of words (in the average case no more than a dozen or so) are your pet demons — words which you and practically no one else misspells.

With the alertness to error that your training has developed in you, you will soon discover such unique errors, if they exist.

Then your skill in visual, kinesthetic, and mnemonic responses to correct patterns will stand you in good stead.

For you now know how to locate the crucial area of any word you misspell —

How to make a complete visual and kinesthetic adjustment to its proper form —

And how to develop a mnemonic for any demon which is particularly troublesome.

In a sense, there is little need to tell you these things.

For, if the intensive training offered in this book has been successful in your case, you will discover and eliminate any further or unique errors not covered by this program — and you will do so without any urging on my part.

You will remain for quite a time visually alert to the appearance in your reading of all the words on which you have trained.

And you will probably discover more errors in printed material, as a result of your training and alertness, than you ever realized existed.

You will then appreciate how nearly expert you have become, how long a stride toward perfection you have taken, how rare an abili you have begun to develop.